To Barry + Sheila –
with love from
Hugo + Caroline    17. 7. 16

# IN VICEREGAL INDIA

*Also edited by David Verney*

The Joyous Patriot: the Correspondence of Ralph Verney,
   1900–1916

# In Viceregal India

## 1916–1921

### *The Letters, Volume 2*

of
Ralph Verney

Edited by
David Verney

TABB HOUSE

First published 1994
Tabb House, 7 Church Street, Padstow, Cornwall PL28 8BG

ISBN 0 907018 93 9

A catalogue record of this title is available from the British Library

Typeset by Exe Valley Dataset Ltd, Exeter
Printed by Short Run Press, Exeter

# *Preface*

Ralph Verney was born in 1879. He joined the Rifle Brigade in 1900, to serve in the Boer War in South Africa as ADC to Lord Chelmsford in Australia. While he was in Sydney, he met and married Nita Walker.

In 1911 Ralph rejoined his regiment in India and was there with his family for three years, until in 1914 his Battalion was posted to France. In 1915 he was wounded at the Battle of Neuve Chapelle and was passed unfit for futher active service.

In 1916 Lord Chelmsford became Viceroy of India. This book begins when Ralph was invited to go out as his Military Secretary, accompanied by Nita and their children John and Jocelyn. The Chelmsfords' children were Joan, born 1895; Frederick, 1896; Anne, 1898; Bridget, 1900; Andrew, 1903; and Margaret, 1911. *In Viceregal India* contains correspondence that deals with the personal aspects of the Verneys' life and it includes letters to Nita and other members of their families as well as some from her.

When Colonel Verney arrived in India he found himself in charge of a staff of 4,000 and responsible for all arrangements for the work and social life of the Viceroy and his family. This was a period when the British Raj was at its height and the ceremony necessary for the maintenance of authority in a vast country is reflected in Ralph's letters. But change was on the way and indeed took place before he left India in 1921. Ghandi and other activists were beginning to make their views felt and echoes of the events that were to detach the British presence from India find their way into these pages.

# Contents

# Acknowledgements

Grateful thanks are due to Lord Knutsford, son of Captain Holland Hibbert, for the use of most of the photographs in this book which his father took while one of Lord Chelmsford's ADCs, and also to Mr Paul Spencer for copying them for reproduction here and to Mrs Joyce Hadley for her proof reading.

# List of Illustrations

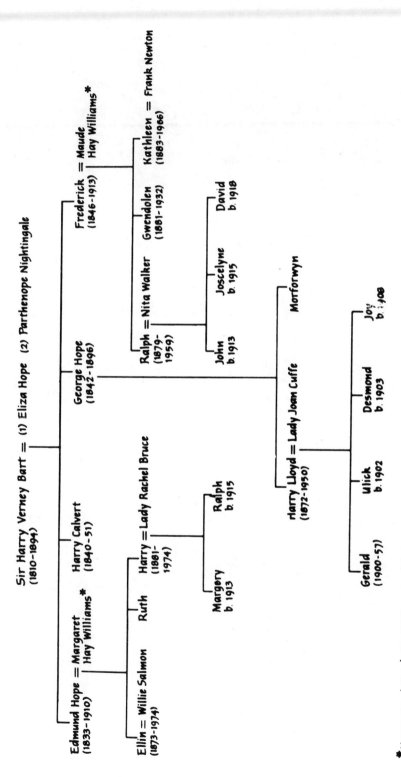

Sir Harry Verney Bart = (1) Eliza Hope  (2) Parthenope Nightingale
(1810–1894)

Edmund Hope = Margaret          Harry Calvert          George Hope          Frederick = Maude
(1833–1910)   Hay Williams*      (1840–51)              (1842–1896)          (1846–1913)  Hay Williams*

Ellin = Willie Salmon    Ruth    Harry = Lady Rachel Bruce                    Ralph = Nita Walker    Gwendolen    Kathleen = Frank Newton
(1873–1974)                      (1881– 1974)                                 (1879– 1959)           (1881–1932)  (1883–1966)

                         Margery    Ralph                                     John      Joscelyne    David
                         b. 1913    b. 1915                                    b. 1913   b. 1915      b. 1918

                                    Harry Lloyd = Lady Joan Cuffe             Morforwyn
                                    (1872–1950)

                         Gerald      Ulick       Desmond      Joy
                         (1900–57)   b. 1902     b. 1903      b. 1908

*Margaret and Maude Hay Williams were sisters

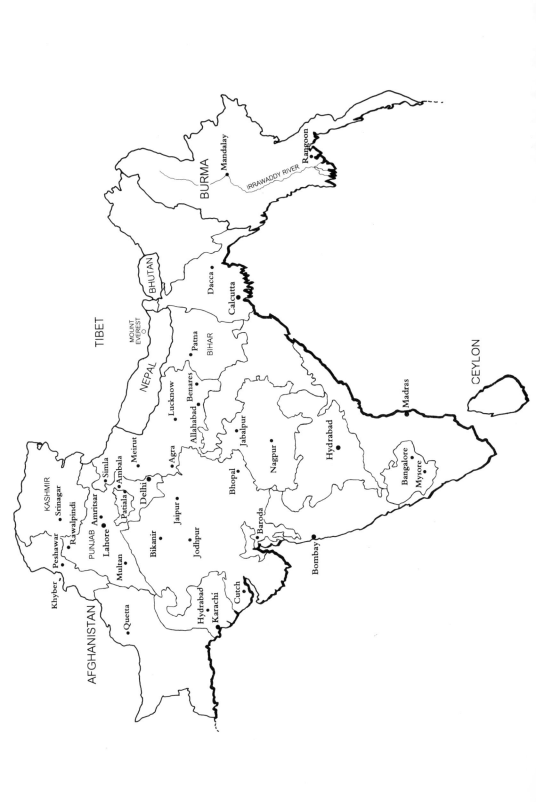

AFGHANISTAN

Khyber
Peshawar
Rawalpindi
KASHMIR
Srinagar
Simla
Ambala
Meirut
PUNJAB
Amritsar
Lahore
Patiala
Delhi
Multan
Quetta
Bikanir
Jaipur
Jodhpur
Hydrabad
Karachi
Cutch
Baroda
Bombay
Bhopal
Nagpur
Jabalpur
Agra
Allahabad
Benares
Lucknow
Patna
BIHAR
Dacca
Calcutta
Hydrabad
Bangalore
Mysore
Madras
CEYLON
TIBET
MOUNT EVEREST
O
NEPAL
BHUTAN
BURMA
Mandalay
IRRAWADDY RIVER
Rangoon

# CHAPTER ONE

Ralph is invited to go to India as his Military Secretary by Lord Chelmsford on his appointment as Viceroy. In March 1916, still only thirty-six years old, Ralph goes to India ahead of the Viceroy. The Viceroy and family and Ralph's wife, Nita, and family follow shortly. After the official reception in Bombay the Viceroy and staff go to Dehra Dun, the Viceroy's retreat outside Delhi, while Nita and family go straight to Simla.

*Lady Chelmsford to Ralph*

January 15th, 1916                    18 Queen's Gate Place
                                              London, S.W.

My dear Ralph,

I have just received a cable from my husband in which he says 'I desire Ralph Verney as military secretary have telegraphed Kitchener will you ask Verney?' So am writing to tell you from him how very much he wishes to have you on his staff, and how much we both hope that you will be able to accept the post which I know you will fill most adequately. It would also be a great pleasure to me to have Nita out in India where she would be a very great help. I do not think you need be anxious about the climate for your children as Simla is cool all the year round and it is always possible to leave them there during the hot weather. My husband always said he intended to have you as his military secretary if he ever became Viceroy of India! And I do not think you will find it easy to go counter to his 'desire'! Come and talk it over with me on Monday.*

                        Yours sincerely,

                      Frances Chelmsford

*Lady Chelmsford was the daughter of Ivor, 1st Lord Wimborne. The family name was Guest.

                    Grant, O Lord, eternal rest
                    Unto thy Servant, Ivor Guest.
                    We do not ask Thee when or how;
                    We only ask Thee, Do it now.

Lord Chelmsford's grandfather was Lord Chancellor of England in 1858 and was made a Baron. His grandson succeeded to the title in 1905 and was vested as Viscount in 1921.

One of his nephews is the famous explorer Wilfred Thesiger.

Lady Chelmsford told Ralph on Monday that it had always been the dream of his life to be Viceroy of India.

*Nita to her mother Mrs Walker in Sydney*

Tuesday, January 18th, 1916                 Queen's Gate Place

I have been busy with Lady C. all the morning, taking the children shopping and to be photographed. Bridget is such a beauty, very tall and graceful; Anne is a big fat lump but jolly and natural. Andrew charming, not in the least shy and so quaint and old-fashioned.[1]

They are all frightfully excited about Lord C.'s new appointment but the younger ones are not in the least keen to go out there; they hate the idea of being Viceregal again.[2]

We were awfully surprised at the appointment and are much excited about it. It is very nice that Ralph should be free these next ten days to be of use to Lady C. I love running round with the children, but Anne and Biddy go back to school tomorrow. Joan is nursing in France. Lord C. left India on Sunday; you know he has been out there for the last eighteen months as a captain in a territorial regiment. I am just going to take Anne out so must stop.

Much love to you all from

Nita

[1]Bridget (Biddy) married Major Richard Sheepshanks in 1919.
   Anne married the 16th Baron Inchiquin in 1921.
   Andrew (1903–1970) succeeded his father as 2nd Viscount in 1933.
[2]Lord Chelmsford had served already as Governor of Queenstown and in New South Wales which perhaps explains the reluctance of his daughters to go to India.

*Ralph to his mother Maude Verney at Botolph Claydon, Bucks*

January 19th, 1916                                    Bachelor's Club, London

My dearest Mother,

I think I may tell you now that Lord Chelmsford has cabled to Lord Kitchener asking for me to go out to India with him as Military Secretary.[1]

I was told yesterday at the War Office that Lord K. had approved of my appointment so I suppose it is more or less settled. I can only say that I feel that it is a very big job for me and that I am most wonderfully lucky to have got such an appointment. I am very busy already arranging innumerable things with Lady C.

Anne is coming to spend a weekend with us; I hope to be able to get home on Friday and will come and see you that evening. I know how pleased Father would have been and I hope you will be pleased too.[2]

I expect to hear from the War Office today or tomorrow when I am to be gazetted.

Your very affectionate

Ralph

[1]Lord Kitchener (1850–1916) was then Secretary of State for War. On June 5th, 1916 he was drowned when HMS *Hampshire* was sunk by a mine in the North Sea.
[2]Anne, Lord Chelmsford's daughter.
 Ralph's father had died in 1913.


*Nita to her father*[1]

Sunday, January 23rd, 1916          Seven Gables, Winslow, Bucks

Dearest Father,
    It is such an honour for Ralph and we are all frightfully pleased; it has just come at the right time. Our tenancy of this house comes to an end on February 28th, Ralph has just been passed unfit by a medical board for active duty and the children are of an age to live in India. Ralph cabled his acceptance to Lord Chelmsford but so far has heard nothing officially from the War Office tho' he heard unofficially from one of Kitchener's secretaries that he approved of the appointment about a week ago. Austen Chamberlain went and saw Lady Chelmsford about it on behalf of the India Office when Lord Chelmsford cabled. Ralph feels quite agitated to think of all these bigwigs discussing him! Whether it comes off or not, it will always be an honour to know that he was asked and was thought worthy of the job by Lord Chelmsford.[2]
    We feel so sure that it will come off we are, or rather I am, making all sorts of preparations, choosing cretonnes, curtains and clothes! We should all travel out together, probably on the *Kaiserihind*, a large P & O which goes to India about March 15th. We shall be such a large party: Lord and Lady Chelmsford, 4 daughters, 3 maids, a house steward, perhaps a chef, 2 if not 3 ADCs, Ralph and I and the family. Nurse and I are getting a maid instead of a nursemaid, who would help Nurse on the voyage and out there maid me; Nurse would have an ayah and a sweeper to attend to the nursery. It all seems like a dream; I can hardly believe it can come to pass. Something will happen to prevent it. It really is

such a perfect plan for tho' it means five years out of England we shall be so much closer to you, and I will be able to take the children perhaps to see you one winter and you might come over to me another winter and escape a Sydney summer. Nurse has not yet decided whether she will come; she is frightened of being drowned or torpedoed, but if we travel with the Chelmsfords they will have an escort. We should only get on board at Marseilles and will pray for rough weather between Marseilles and Port Said. They cannot do much harm in rough weather; it is the lesser of the two evils! After Port Said there are no dangers. But with an armed escort of cruisers, etc., we wouldn't be attacked. I am enclosing a copy of a very nice letter Lady Chelmsford wrote Ralph. He will have a lot of hard work as military secretary. The staff consists of a Private Secretary and Assistant P. Secretary who are Indian Civil Servants. Mr Maffey, the private secretary, is a very well-known man and his wife I believe is charming.

Under Ralph is the Comptroller of the Household, about 4 ADCs, the Viceroy's Bodyguard and their officers and, so Ralph has been told, but we can hardly believe it, 4,000 servants!! and employees!! We don't know whether he will get a house or not but according to Whitaker the MS's salary is £1,200 a year.

Much love to you all,

Nita

[1]Nita's father Senator Walker was one of the six Senators chosen to draw up the Constitution of Australia and it was he who suggested Canberra as the Capital City.
[2]Austen Chamberlain (1863–1937) was Secretary of State for India from December 10th, 1916 to July 17th, 1917, when he was succeeded by Edwin Montagu.

*Nita to her mother*

February 2nd, 1916                                    Marylebone Road

Darling Mumpty,

Lord Chelmsford arrived today with Lady C. who went to meet him at Marseilles. He was so nice to Ralph and told him he was so delighted that he was going to have his services again. He wants him to go out on the ship before him and make arrangements for his arrival at Bombay. I shall probably go on the *Kaiserihind* with the Chelmsford party because it is to be escorted and will be the bigger and quicker boat.[1]

Ralph is having a most interesting time; he spent two hours at the India Office on Monday and had half an hour's chat with Austen Chamberlain whom he thought delightful; the other hour and a half was split up between Gen. Sir Edmund Barrow and Sir Dunlop Smith, both bigwigs in the India Office who were most charming and helpful. He is to dine on February 24th, with Austen Chamberlain; a small dinner he is giving Lord Chelmsford; the rest of the guests are all Cabinet Ministers, the India Office men I've just mentioned and some important Indians who are over here.[2]

Much love from

Nita

[1] Lord Chelmsford had returned from India where he had been serving in the Army.
[2] General Sir Edmund Barrow (1852–1934) was the Military Secretary at the India Office. He had previously raised and commanded the Hong Kong Regiment.

Sir James Robert Dunlop Smith (1858–1921) had been Private Secretary to the Earl of Minto, Viceroy of India 1905–1910.

*Ralph to Nita's father*

February 18th, 1916                              Seven Gables, Winslow

My dear Daddy,

My duties as Military Secretary are fairly numerous; I am Head of the Staff except for the Private Secretary, have to keep the ADCs up to their work, am responsible for the running and payment of the household, though the Comptroller does most of that under me; have to manage all the correspondence with native chiefs, have to arrange all tours, also all parades attended by the Viceroy and have to manage about a dozen funds, such as the touring fund, the fund for keeping up and improving the Viceregal gardens and residences in India, the stable fund, etc. etc., and I have always to be with the Viceroy driving in his carriage or riding at his elbow![1]

I am sure I shall find it exceedingly interesting, but am only very anxious not to make a hash of the job! I think I told you I get £1,200 a year and a house, so I am certainly well paid.

During the last three weeks I have had talks with a good many interesting people, including Austen Chamberlain and Lord Stamfordham, the King's private secretary, and Col. Clive Wigram, the assistant private secretary.

I am to get the rank of Lt. Col. the day I take over my duties in India. All this means a good deal of expense what with clothes for Nita, uniforms, and our passages; this will come to at least £600, but as I am well paid out there I can afford this outlay, and one must have an outfit which will do for the next five years.

I get to Bombay on March 25th and stay for a day or two with the Willingdons at Government House there, then go on to Delhi and stay with the Viceroy for a few days, when I try and learn as much as I can from Frank Maxwell, the present Military Secretary, and then return to Bombay to meet the Chelmsfords on the April 3rd.[2]

We all go to Delhi that evening and they will stay for a day or two at Delhi before going to Dehra Dun, a country bungalow about sixty miles from Delhi, for about a fortnight, during which time Lord C. goes for a short visit to Calcutta, staying with Lord Carmichael. I doubt if I shall go there as I shall be busy fixing up the household in Simla ready for them to come into residence there about the middle of April.[3]

I don't know whether Nita and the family will go straight up to Simla; perhaps they will stay at Dehra Dun too, but I shall have to see what is best for them when I arrive.

Your very affectionate

Ralph

*Ralph's previous service with his regiment in India was of enormous help to him.
†Freeman Freeman-Thomas, 1st Marquess of Willingdon (1886–1941) was Governor of Bombay, 1913–19, of Madras 1919–24, Governor-General of Canada 1926–31, Viceroy and Governor-General of India 1931–36.
  Colonel Francis Maxwell (1871–1917) was Military Secretary to Lord Hardinge, Viceroy of India 1910–16. He won the Victoria Cross at Korn Spruit in the Boer War in March, 1900.
‡Thomas David Gibson-Carmichael, 14th Bart and 1st Baron (1859–1926), had been Governor of Victoria, Australia 1908–11, of Madras 1911–12 and was Governor of Bengal 1912–17.

*Ralph to his mother*

March 8th, 1916                                    33 Manor House,
                                              Marylebone Road N.W.

My dear Mother

This last year has been a most happy one for us all; I could not
have believed a year ago that I should be spared to be with my
family for a whole year.

Mind you take every care of yourself especially in this cold damp
weather. I had a very nice letter from Lister Kaye; perhaps you will
see him when you go to Pleasley.*

Your very affectionate son,

Ralph

*Pleasley is a 15,000 acre agricultural estate in Derbyshire, with coal mines
underneath, left to Ralph's father, and so to Ralph, by Florence Nightingale.

*Ralph to Nita*

March 12th, 1916                    Grand Hotel de la Paix, Marseilles

My own Darling,

I arrived here about 4 p.m. today and Amoradat met me at the
station with the news that our boat has been delayed and will not
arrive here till Tuesday, so here I am for two nights; it is annoying
as there is nothing to do and it means we shall be three days late
the other end. The same thing of course may happen to you, but if
not I shall have a very short time to do all I want to do.*

Very much love to you all, your own husband,

Ralph

*A Siamese Prince in the Siamese Embassy in Paris. Ralph's father had acted for
many years as adviser to the Siamese Royal family.

March 14th, 1916                    Grand Hotel de la Paix, Marseilles

My own Darling,

My boat came in this morning and we leave at 5 p.m. I do hope you will not have this delay, but I expect not, though most of the Mail Boats lately have been one or two days late. The P & O Company gives passengers £1 a day for being delayed here to pay for our hotel expenses.

Your own husband

Ralph

March 15th, 1916                                        S.S. *Kashgar*

My own Darling,

We finally left Marseilles about 3 a.m. this morning. I did not hear us start. It simply poured with rain all yesterday afternoon which delayed the loading up of this ship.

I have been talking to General Hunter Blair who is a brother of Lady Glasgow's and consequently uncle to Lady Alice Fergusson and the Boyles. The General's brother lives next door to Kilkurran where I stayed for shooting and his sister-in-law walked over and had tea with us on the Sunday. He is going to Malta having got a job there. He sent all his personal belongings including linen, etc., on the *Maloja* and so lost everything he possessed. We have on board a Naval Commander who was onboard her and who was picked up after being about forty-five minutes in the water.*

Ralph

*Major-General Walter Hunter-Blair (1860–1938) was GOC Malta 1915–19. His sister, Dorothea, was married to the 7th Earl of Glasgow who had been Governor of New Zealand 1892–97. Their daughter, Lady Alice Boyle, was married to General Sir Charles Fergusson who was Governor-General of New Zealand 1924–30.

*Ralph to his mother*

March 20th, 1916                                  S.S. *Kashgar*

My dearest Mother,

We are due at Port Said in a few hours and I am glad to say our trip so far has been without any unfortunate incident. At Malta I saw Lord Methuen who is such a charming old man; I also saw his Military Secretary, Col. Radcliffe, and Lord Windsor who is ADC. I thought him quite nice but he has something of his mother's cold manner and did not seem to be quite as thrilled as he might have been at meeting me!! especially as I explained that his father was my godfather.*

Nita ought to arrive in Malta tomorrow morning unless she has been also delayed; I shall hear in Port Said when they left Marseilles.

Very much love, your very affectionate

Ralph

*Lord Methuen (1845–1932) had commanded the 1st Division of the 1st Army Corps in the Boer War. He was defeated by Kronje et Magersfontein and later (1902) taken prisoner by De La Rey. Commander-in-Chief South Africa 1907–09, Governor of Malta 1915–19.

Ivor Miles Windsor-Clive (1889–1943), Lord Windsor, later 2nd Earl of Plymouth.

*Ralph to Nita's father*

March 27th, 1916                                  S.S. *Salsette*

My dear Daddy,

I got your letter yesterday at Aden, and very pleased I was to hear from you. I did not get any letters at Port Said, so Nita will find them there; I got a wire from her yesterday from Port Said, so I am much relieved and feel no more anxiety about them.

Mr Maffey, who is to be Private Secretary, was at Aden waiting for Lord Chelmsford, so we met and had a good long talk together; I liked him very much indeed; he is very tall, about 6ft. 3in., and has four children, the fourth having made its appearance two days ago.[1]

I am staying in Bombay with the Willingdons and their Military Secretary is meeting me with a launch; the Hardinge party arrive at Bombay on Saturday so I shall have three clear days with Maxwell, to get as many tips from him as I can; he wrote to me to Aden, that he would fix up for Nita and the family to go straight up to Simla; I think this is much the best plan really, as Bombay and Delhi will be pretty hot; the Chelmsfords will land about 8 a.m. and there will be a pretty big function, guards of honour, streets lined with troops etc.[2]

Lord C., Lord Willingdon, myself and Greig, the Bombay Military Secretary, are in the first carriage; Lady C., Lady W., and 2 ADCs in the second and then the girls and the rest of the party in the other carriages; I doubt if Nita will be in the procession though I daresay she will go on shore early so as to see it.[3]

Yours very affectionately,

Ralph

[1]John Leader Maffey (1877–1969) was made KCVO in 1921, KCMG 1931, KCB 1934, GCMG 1935, and 1st Baron Rugby in 1947. He was Private Secretary to the Viceroy 1916–20; Chief Secretary to the Duke of Connaught 1921; Governor-General of the Sudan 1926–33; Permanent Under-Secretary of State for the Colonies 1933–37.
[2]Charles, 1st Baron Hardinge of Penshurst (1858–1944) had been Lord Chelmsford's predecessor as Viceroy of India (1910–16). He later (1920–23) became Ambassador to France.
[3]The Rev. Lt-Col John Greig (1871–1958) was Military Secretary to Lord Willingdon 1913–18. He was ordained as a Roman Catholic priest in Rome in 1935 and became President of Hampshire County Cricket Club in 1945.

*Nita to her family*

March 28th, 1916                                   S.S. *Kaiserihind*

Darling Family,

You will be longing to hear all about this voyage. In some ways it has been the jolliest I've ever done, in others ghastly. The babies have been very bad travellers; John dreadfully train sick all the way from Boulogne to Marseilles and consequently very over excited and unlike himself. The baby has shrieked and yelled herself hoarse until the day we reached Port Said; since then she has had a very bad cough and high temperature. Nurse and I have not had a moment's sleep for about three nights and neither of us can sleep in the daytime. Last night I had to get the doctor for her at three, her temperature went up in such an alarming way; he gave her a strong sleeping draught but it had no effect so she is still wailing. Everyone has been most kind and are so ready to help. Poor Biddy has been in floods of tears over it because it was she who gave her the cold originally. She is such a delightful child. Very tall and graceful, about 5 ft. 9 in., so pretty but perfectly natural, not in the least self-conscious or flirtatious; she is nearly sixteen. Anne is plain but very unselfish and good natured, always doing everyone else's dirty jobs; Joan is most fascinating, very vivacious, a great chatterbox and so pretty. Lord and Lady C. mix with everyone and are most gracious to all and sundry, take part in our games. The rest of our party consists of Sir George Barnes, one of the Viceroy's council, a perfect old dear whom we all call Cousin George. He is very clever and has been working at the Board of Trade with Mr Runciman since war broke out; it was he who bought in the world's supply of sugar when war broke out and he told me he has just done another deal with Scandinavia and bought all their fish and oil which will be a dreadful blow to Germany. His wife is not coming out for several months so he is taking out a most beautiful cousin of hers to be his hostess, Margaret Abel-Smith. She is also Ralph's second cousin but doesn't know him. She is twenty-nine or thirty. Another cousin of hers is our youngest ADC, Capt. Holland-Hibbert; he is a nephew of Lord Knutsford, generally known as Sydney Holland. I've never met a nicer boy for his age; he is twenty-three, 6 ft. 4in., very nice looking and clean shaven, the type of Englishman I like so much, very straight and clean with a high ideal for men and women. He has travelled a lot and is so well read. He has been serving in the Herts Yeomanry since war broke out but his heart is weak so he has to give up soldiering.*

Much love to you all,

Nita

*Joan Thesiger was the Chelmsfords' eldest daughter. In 1920 she married Alan Lascelles, nephew of the 5th Earl of Harewood. The letters and journals of Sir Alan Lascelles, who became ADC to the Governor of Bombay in 1919, were published in 1986 under the title *End of an Era*.

Sir George Barnes (1858–1946) was a Member of the Council of the Viceroy of India 1916–21. The 'perfect old dear's' only recorded publication was entitled *Handbook of the Death Duties*.

Walter (later (1937) 1st Viscount) Runciman (1870–1949) was President of the Board of Trade 1914–16. He was, between 1899 and 1937, Liberal MP for Oldham, Dewsbury, Swansea and St Ives.

Margaret Abel-Smith married, 1924, Sir Herbert Palmer who was Governor of Cyprus 1933–39. Her mother, also called Margaret, was the 2nd daughter of the 1st Viscount Knutsford.

Wilfrid (Biffy) Holland-Hibbert (1893–1961) later became Estates Bursar to Merton College, Oxford, and a Governor of the Royal Agricultural College, Cirencester.

*Ralph to his mother*

March 31st, 1916                         Government House, Bombay

My dearest Mother,

I got here this morning early and Greig, the military secretary, met me onboard with a special launch and brought me to Government House in a motor, in time for breakfast. This is a most glorious house and everything very Viceregal!

Tomorrow morning we are having a sort of undress rehearsal for the ceremony on Tuesday; the troops were practising it here this morning when I arrived.

I am going onboard early by myself in the launch about 7 a.m., a few officials come about a quarter of an hour later and then we disembark at 8 a.m. A huge marquee is being built on the quay where Lord C. arrives, and he holds a reception there first. Many of the Indian chiefs have come to Bombay to receive him, also members of the Council, etc. Lord and Lady Willingdon are coming tomorrow morning to this rehearsal and I am to accompany them.

Your very affectionate

Ralph

April 6th, 1916                 Viceregal Lodge, Delhi

My dearest Mother,

Here I am in my Military Secretary's office which is in a large double tent fitted out with telephones, electric light and fans, etc. My own secretary, an excellent man called Parsons, is in the next tent with clerks in other tents beyond.

We had a very good journey up here from Bombay and the Viceroy's train is most comfortable. I and the private secretary have large compartments to ourselves with writing desks fitted up, and we each have our secretarial departments with us on the train and also a post office.

We had a state arrival this morning and there were a good many officials to receive them on arrival at Viceregal Lodge. Errington and I drove up with the Chelmsfords in the first carriage surrounded by the bodyguard; there were four carriages in the procession. Today most of the officials of the government have been paying official calls on HE but I have been sitting all day in this office and have just about finished now. A copy of every telegram that is sent out by or received by Army Headquarters is sent to me for my information, I sort them out and any of importance or interest I send on by my orderly to HE who initials them and sends them back to me again. So I am the first person to hear news of Mesopotamia, etc., which is of course most interesting.[1]

The C-in-C, his military secretary and ADC lunched here today. Tomorrow night we go on to Dehra Dun by train arriving there Saturday morning early. On Sunday night I go off to Calcutta with HE, Maffey the private secretary and one ADC: this will be a very hot trip. We get back to Dehra Dun the following Saturday morning and I shall then hope to go on to join Nita at Simla, arriving there midday on Sunday. I shall have from Sunday to Wednesday there before the Chelmsfords arrive, which will be delightful as I have not seen anything of Nita and the children for so long.

Did you hear of the frightfully narrow shave they had in the Mediterranean when a torpedo missed them by fifty feet? It happened at 7 a.m. on the morning after they left Malta. The officer on the bridge most luckily saw it coming from some way off and quickened the pace of the ship immediately and so the torpedo passed fifty feet behind the ship. It was entirely owing to the fault of the commander of the two destroyers escorting them who gave orders to the Captain of the *Kaiserihind* to sail a straight course instead of zig-zagging because he said there was no risk at all; however after this narrow escape he cancelled that order and they zigzagged the rest of the way to Port Said. I am glad to say that Lord C. reported the matter to the Admiral at Port Said. I was absolutely horrified when I heard about it, but Nita took it quite calmly and said she was quite prepared to do part of the trip in the water when she left home!!

*Later*

I have just rung up Simla and am afraid Nita and the children had a terrible escape; they were nearly killed and poor Nita, as you will know, is about as good as anyone I know in an emergency, was quite overcome on arrival. I have been talking to the doctor who was called in at once; he tells me that Nita is sleeping as peacefully as the children and he feels sure that she will be perfectly all right when she wakes up. But he is going to telephone to me again about 8 p.m. The children are both absolutely all right and as well as possible. The nurse is very tired out too. I am telephoning to the Railway authorities to send me a full report of the accident in view of the fact that Their Ex.s propose to do the same trip on the 20th. I did not send you a wire about their arrival, but I shall do so tomorrow morning if they are all well.

You can imagine what my feelings were when I first heard of the accident. HE kindly offered to let me go off tonight straight away to Simla but I shall not do so if the report of the doctor at 8 p.m. is satisfactory, but if he thinks that my presence up there is desirable I shall take heed of HE's offer.[2]

Your very affectionate son

Ralph

[1]Viscount Errington (1877–1953), later 2nd Earl of Cromer, had been ADC to Lord Hardinge 1915–16. His wife, Ruby, was the daughter of the Earl of Minto who had been Viceroy of India 1905–10.

[2]*Account by Nita:*

We had two nights in the train and two very long days. We reached Kalka at 5 one morning and came up here in a motor which runs along the railway line, but owing to a breakdown didn't get here till 4.30; we were due at 12. Owing to this breakdown we had to get out and walk, Nurse carrying Joscelyne and I John. We had two miles to go and three tunnels to go thro', one a quarter of a mile long. It wasn't jolly. We got here tired out and all went to bed.

*Ralph to Nita*

April 7th, 1916                                    Viceregal Lodge, Delhi

My own Darling,

I can think of little else but your wonderful escape yesterday. I had a most horrid fright for a short time, but nothing to what you must have had. I am so distressed to think of the difficult time you had carrying those children all that way; I hope that you have given a word account of it all to the railway inspector, or will do so if he has not called on you already. I talked to him very straight on the telephone last night and brought to bear all the weight of the Military Secretary to the Viceroy!!!

You know how I am longing to get up to you. I'm so awfully glad that you are so pleased with the house, it makes such a difference as it will be our home for the next five years, more or less. I went through the tents which will be ours here; I thought they seemed quite comfortable. I will have one more put up for the maid; you realise there will only be one for the nurse and children to use day and night, but by putting Pick [the maid] into another one, I can have two tents, one for the day and one for the night. We shall have a bed- and dressing-room and dining-room with one tent across the road for any guest. My office here can act as our bankers here if you like and will pay all our bills, household ones and private ones; it will save you a lot of bother.

More papers and more telegrams are just coming in; I must deal with them now as this office closes tonight.

Very much love dearest heart, take every care of your precious self and the children,

Your own husband,

Ralph

April 8th, 1916            Viceroy's Camp, India
Dehra Dun

My own Darling,

We arrived here at 8 a.m. this morning, and I came up in the motor with Their Ex.s to this bungalow which is about three miles from the station. There was a guard paraded by the 2nd Gurkhas who made no preparation for having a warning given them of the approach of the motor and so, when we did come along, all the men were just standing at ease and the officer did not salute at all. I sent an ADC for him at once and asked him the reason; the only excuse he could give me was that the motor car came quicker than he expected. I wrote a note to the Colonel about it who sent up his adjutant to apologise profusely for it; who do you think this adjutant was? Corse Scott!! He and his wife are both here and I have got Their Ex.s to ask them both to dinner tonight and I have instructed Sykes, who is in waiting today, to put me next to Mrs Corse Scott at dinner!!

This is a most delightful place, and it all looks so green after Delhi; it is much cooler than Delhi. Lady C. has already rather got up on her hind legs about having people presented to her at the station and also she insists on us all addressing her as Her Excellency or Your Excellency and never as Lady C. I have had to inform the staff to this effect. I am getting a little bit doubtful as to whether I shall be able to get away from here on Saturday next but I shall try my best to do so.

Very much love,

Your own Ralph

April 9th, 1916            Viceroy's Camp, India
Dehra Dun

My own Darling,

We had a little dinner party last night and I gave instructions to the staff that every formality that would be observed in the case of a large dinner party should be gone through with this one. I did this because Sykes and Hibbert were both on duty and I wanted them to try their hand at it for the first time; it all went off quite well and I think they will both have more confidence in themselves next time. I let Hibbert off duty in the afternoon as he was very anxious to try a polo pony, and I took Her Ex. and Anne out in the motor to some sports that were being held on the race course; I think she really quite enjoyed them and ended up by giving away the prizes. His Ex. who was riding with Joan and Sykes turned up at them for a short time.

I have had a busy morning. I did not go to church which was at 7.30, but directly after breakfast I took one of the motors and went to inspect the stables here which are about three miles away, though of course we have got standing for a few horses here in the grounds. After that I went on to the Bodyguard which I inspected thoroughly with Capt. de Gale, the four Indian officers were presented to me and after touching the hilts of their swords I shook hands with each of them; at the end of my inspection I asked de Gale to express to them my complete satisfaction with everything I had seen and to say that I was especially pleased with the grooming of each and every horse, which was really excellent. I also told them that the Viceroy would come and inspect them personally immediately on his return from Calcutta. I think they were all pleased because de Gale told me that though they had all worked extremely hard to make a fine show on the occasion of Lord Hardinge's departure, Maxwell had forgotten to write or express any appreciation of their efforts on behalf of Lord Hardinge. I am therefore going to be careful and send a complimentary order to them after the present Viceroy has inspected them, which I hope will be next Saturday evening.*

Your own husband,

Ralph

*Hugh Otway de Gale (1891–1966) was then serving in the Indian Army. He later joined the Indian Police and became Inspector-General of Police NWFP 1935–41.

# CHAPTER TWO

In April 1916 the Viceroy goes on his first official tour
to Calcutta. Nita sets up house in Simla. The Viceroy
returns to Dehra Dun and then goes up to Simla. Life
in Simla and in Mashobra, the Viceregal retreat from
Simla.

April 11th, 1916                    Government House, Calcutta

My own Darling,

We had a very good journey here and it was not really too hot, nor at the present moment is it hot in Calcutta but it is rather sticky. Sir James Meston came to see HE at Lucknow for ten minutes or so. Lord Suffolk who was to have come in the train with us missed his connection somewhere and so never got to Laksar in time to join us there. I got a telegram from him later on to say that he had been 'hung up' but whether on a motor or a train or a gallows I do not know! Lord Carmichael met us at the station; I drove up in the car with Their Exs.[1]

I sent you a telegram this morning to say that we were prosperous. I really do not know yet what day I can come to you. I am engaging accommodation for Sunday night, reaching you early Monday, but it all depends if important telegrams are still coming in from Mesopotamia. If things are still critical there I do not think I ought to be away from HE as I have to show him sometimes where places are on the map and also sometimes draft out some telegram or other which he wants to send; I shall telegraph you if I can get away or not. We have got an inspection of the Bodyguard on Saturday afternoon.

This House looks perfectly huge, a sort of Hampton Court Palace as one drives up to it, but I believe there are not many rooms in it really and they cannot put up very many people at a time. There is a beautiful big dining-room with a floor of dark green marble, pillars of white marble and a Silver Throne in the throne room at the end of it. The Silver Throne belonged to Warren Hastings. It does strike one as so curious coming along in the Viceroy's train to see the line guarded the whole way by policemen on each side. The whole way from Bombay to Delhi, and from there to Dehra Dun and then the whole way to Calcutta, were men standing about 200 yards apart with their backs to the line and armed with long sticks some of which had a sort of scythe blade fixed onto the end of it, at night many of them carrying flaming torches. These men are not all belonging to the regular police but are chowkidars or local village men who are taken on for the day and are just paid 3 or 4 annas for the job.[2]

1. Lt Col. Ralph Verney in his viceregal uniform, aged 38

2. Nita Verney, Ralph's wife, and daughter of Senator Hon. J.T. Walker of Sydney

3. The Viceroy of India, 1st Viscount Chelmsford

4. The Vicereine, Lady Chelmsford

1916. H.E. the Viceroy's arrival at Bombay. Lord and Lady
Chelmsford (centre of group, Viceroy in dark suit); Hon. Joan
Thesiger (facing camera, left), Hon. A. Thesiger, right; Ralph
Verney at edge of steps. See p. 21

6.  H.E.'s carriage leaving Bombay for Government House

7.  H.E. with senior Staff and and Indian Princes

6 April 1916.

*[shorthand symbols]*

Parsons

Bombay

Viceroy's

secretarial

Vice Regal Lodge

Errington        Chelmsford —

Body Guard

8. One of Ralph's shorthand letters

His Ex. has travelled in his train during this last week 1875
miles, so working it out at 10 men on each side of the line per mile
or 20 men per mile, that means that 37,500 men have been on duty
guarding the railway for him during this last week. It is exactly a
week since I met you on the *Kaiserihind*; I really have seen nothing
of you at all yet but do not expect to till I get to Simla.

Your own

Ralph

[1]Sir James (later 1st Baron) Meston (1865–1943) was Lt-Governor United
Provinces, Agra and Oudh 1912–18.
  The 19th Earl of Suffolk and Berkshire (1877–1917) was killed in action.
He had been ADC to Lord Curzon, Viceroy of India, 1899–1905. His wife,
Marguerite, was the sister of Lord Curzon's first wife, Mary. Their maiden name
was Leiter, hence Mary's nickname 'The Leiter of Asia', when Vicereine.
[2]Warren Hastings (1732–1818) was created Governor-General of India in 1773.
He was impeached for corruption and cruelty in his administration of India in
1788, but was acquitted after a famous trial in which Burke and Sheridan were
among the prosecuting counsel.

*Nita to Ralph's mother*

April 13th, 1916                           Viceregal Lodge, Simla

My dear Mother,
   When we reached Bombay I was dressed and at the top of the
gangway waiting for Ralph to come on board at 6 a.m. He made his
appearance at 6.30; I had him to myself for about ten minutes. He
told me to my great surprise that I was to go ashore with all the
family and take part in the procession; the children were to go to the
house of some friend of the Willingdons. I enjoyed it all immensely,
especially as Joscelyne was so very much better. We landed at 8 and
were received on the top of the steps by the Willingdons who then
walked into a huge tent packed with important people, Indian chiefs
in wonderful jewels and silks, leading Bombay men and women. The
Chelmsfords took their seat upon a small dais in the middle of the
tent and about 100 people were brought up and introduced. The
girls and I could not help admiring the man who announced them
all; he never referred to any notes but rolled out the names of
Hindus, Mohammedans and Parsees with the greatest ease, and

some of the latter were tongue-twisters. The President of the Bombay Municipal Council read out an address to which HE replied; he looked every inch the Viceroy as he stood before them. I think it was a very thrilling moment for both HE and Lady C. We took our seats in the carriage when that was all over; I was in the fourth with Anne and Bridget, Ralph in the first with HE and Lord Willingdon. The drive through the streets of Bombay was a great experience; the sky was brilliant blue as only a tropical sky can be, the buildings a dazzling white and we drove through vast crowds of every kind, the Indians in such brilliant coloured clothes that stood out so well against the white bungalows. They cheered most spontaneously; I loved every minute of it.

The carriage drive up to Government House is most unique, the drive is bordered on one side by the open sea, on the other by quite a dense jungle. Our escort and bodyguard were magnificently turned out, all picked men.

Lord Hardinge and his staff received us at the top of the steps of Gov. House; we all thought he looked so tired and sad. We returned to Gov. House for lunch, a rather memorable gathering as Lord Hardinge and staff and Lord Chelmsford and staff were all there together; there were some other guests as well. Afterwards we had a group taken and Lord Hardinge said goodbye and drove off to the ship with the Bodyguard.

The Chelmsfords had several things to do after that and Ralph had to go in attendance, so I had to say goodbye and take my party off to the station. We were two nights and two and a half days in the train and the heat as far as Kalka was very trying. From Kalka to Simla we travelled up in a motor on lines. The views going up were too lovely and I longed for someone to tell me the names of all the lovely flowering shrubs we passed.

Viceregal Lodge has several acres of grounds and all the married staff have houses in these grounds; we are about half an hour by rickshaw from the Mall, the principal shopping quarter and from the majority of houses. Sir George Barnes and Margaret Abel-Smith are nearly an hour's drive by rickshaw.

Our servants wear most gorgeous red and gold livery supplied by the comptroller; most of them are paid by him too. This is what our staff consists of:

1. Cook with cook's mate and under cook 3
2. Dhobi or washerman 1
3. Bearer, Ralph's personal Servant 1
4. Head Kitmagar, table servant 1
5. Under Kitmagar 1
6. 2 Champrassis, messengers, one is always on duty to answer the telephone 2
7. One Khalassi, housemaid 1
8. 1 Sweeper 1
9. 1 Bhisti water-carrier 1
10. One Mali and two mates, gardener and boys, we have two beds to look after 3
11. One Ayah, nurse 1
12. One Nursery maid to push prams as no woman can get it up the hills 1
13. Four Shampanis or rickshaw men 4
14. 2 or 3 Syce or grooms to look after our horses for riding 3
Total: 24

This would be our complete staff, and we have a house not only so large as The Seven Gables, four rooms including Pick's bedroom downstairs, five rooms upstairs; one of the downstairs rooms was a bedroom but I have turned it into a cosy room for Ralph.

Ever your affectionate daughter,
Nita


*Ralph to Nita*

April 13th, 1916                                    Viceroy's Camp, India
                                                              Calcutta

My own Darling,

Yesterday evening we had a big evening garden party. Unfortunately heavy rain fell at 8 p.m. so that the first part of it was held inside after the guests had arrived. A procession was formed of the staff, and the Governor and Viceroy came the whole length of the large dining-room with the marble floor and went up onto the dais. His Ex. presented a few medals and then about twenty Indian officers were brought up; he touched the hilts of their swords which were offered to him by each as he came up and then shook hands with each of them. After that various people were brought up to him, and then as it was fine and the room dreadfully crowded, I suggested to him that he should make a move out into the garden which he did and everybody followed.

I met your cousin Lyon yesterday morning and evening and again this morning; he would appeal to your father very much I think. Last night when His Ex. wanted to come in, Lord Carmichael could not be found anywhere, having quite safely hidden himself away from any of his staff with a very pretty Maharani. However he was eventually found and brought HE upstairs. HE said 'well I expect you will be going to bed now, good night,' to which Lord C. replied 'yes certainly; good night,' but Maffey who came in a few minutes later met him on his way out again into the garden in pursuit of other fairies!!*

Yesterday afternoon we started off about 5 p.m. to visit various institutions such as the Tropical School of Medicine, the University Institute, etc. We went through what is supposed to be a most dangerous part of Calcutta; I will tell you about the warning I was given in the morning when I meet you; but everything went off very well indeed and after getting back here about 6 p.m. I went out just for a drive with HE and Lady C. round the Maidan and race-course.

This morning we started off at 7.45 to visit the Victoria Memorial which is being built and which is costing about half a million; it will not be finished for the next six years. On our return here HE inspected a small ambulance company before breakfast.

He has interviews most of this morning; I am going out to return a few calls on various Rajahs, etc. We have a garden party at the Calcutta Club this afternoon, a dinner party this evening and then start back in our train at 10.30 p.m.

Your own
Ralph

*Lord Carmichael, the Governor of Bengall

April 17th, 1916					Viceroy's Camp, India
					Dehra Dun

My own Darling

I got up at 5.30 this morning and went out shooting with Maffey and Bramley who is a police inspector of sorts: quail; we got 38 brace, 2 hares and a cat. I shot the latter in mistake for a hare; it was a wild cat and had been eating young quail so it was quite a good thing to shoot it. We are going out again on Wednesday morning, it really is quite good fun once one is up! We got back here about 9.15 a.m

This afternoon the de Gales are taking Joan and Anne Sykes and Hibbert out to stay in the jungle for a night, about twenty miles from here, and are going to sit up in machans [hides] and watch wild animals come to drink both this evening and very early tomorrow morning. Tomorrow afternoon there is a gymkhana given by the 2nd Gurkhas which Their Ex.s are going to. This morning the Maharajah of Udaipur has been to pay a call on HE; we had a guard of honour here and two ADCs in white uniform to meet him.

The Indian in charge of the Post Office came to see me this morning and told me that our best address always, no matter where we were, is Viceroy's Camp, India. You might tell your people this; the letters if addressed like this, with no place mentioned at all, come straight to the Viceroy's own Post Office. I do not know whether you post your letters at Vice Regal Lodge; it is the best thing for you to do as the letters are put straight away into the bag, sealed up and delivered there at once without going to any other Post Office at all.

Your own

Ralph

April 18th, 1916                                          Viceroy's Camp, India
                                                                    Dehra Dun

My own Darling,

Every Indian official who has any connection at all with this house or the grounds seems to have been to pay his respects to me these last few days, such as the Indian in charge of the buildings, the Indian in charge of the grounds, the Indian police inspector and this morning the Indian doctor whose duty it seems to be to go round and inspect the latrines!! They all produce innumerable letters of recommendation from former members of the staff and give me a history of their own careers from the date of their birth up to the present day. Also every morning two Gurkha officers come to my room about 10 a.m., salute me with a tremendous flourish and gabble some report about the sentries guarding this place. I try to look as if I understood and murmur 'Acha' which seems to satisfy them as they again salute with the same flourish and retire. Yesterday a very young subaltern who has only been here for three weeks came in charge of the guard for the visit of the Maharajah of Udaipur; he had not to command them but was sent just to see that they took up their proper positions, etc., so I brought him along to my room and gave him the latest telegrams to read. He was an awfully nice boy but awfully frightened of me at first!! However when he left I hope he had decided that the military secretary was not really very alarming.

This afternoon we are going to the regimental sports of the 2nd Gurkhas. I rather think they have arranged for them to take place now so as to get Their Ex.s to attend them. Maffey and I are going to motor over and dine quietly with the de Gales tonight; I wrote a letter to him after the inspection of the Bodyguard which pleased him very much, saying that His Ex. had been particularly struck by the smart appearance of the men at drill and that he considered that the grooming of the horses deserved special notice, etc. HE was rather amused at the letter when I showed it to him and said he was glad to read of the things he was supposed to have specially noticed at the inspection!

Very much love,
Your own husband,

Ralph

*Ralph to his mother*

April 21st, 1916                                    Viceregal Lodge, Simla

My dearest Mother,

We arrived up here yesterday about midday and there was a large crowd to be presented to Their Ex.s including the C-in-C and practically all the headquarters staff. This was to have taken place on the lawn outside but there had been a good deal of rain so it was too wet underfoot, all the presentations therefore took place in the ballroom; I did not see Nita until after we had inspected the Guard of Honour and had come inside the house, but she was up on a balcony watching this part of the proceedings with John; she then came down and was in the smaller of the drawing-rooms with a few other people as we passed through. The whole show was over in about half an hour and I went home to lunch. Our house is quite charming and Nita has worked awfully hard to make it nice. It is much more like an English house than any I have seen out here; it isn't a bungalow at all but a proper brick house with a delightful hall and staircase and many scarlet-clothed orderlies waiting about just inside the front door which has a porch.

I have got a most delightful den in which Nita has got a writing table too. The champrassi or orderly goes to my house every morning early just in order to put fresh blotting-paper on the table, to see that the writing paper desk is full and pencils, pens, etc., are in proper order. I am now writing at my office at Viceregal Lodge which is just as grand as a manager's office at home. Two scarlet-clothed champrassis stand outside my door ready to take papers, messages, telegrams, etc., I have got private telephones to the Viceroy's room, Private Secretary, Military Secretary to the C-in-C, etc. etc.; also anybody ringing me up from anywhere whether it is here or in Delhi, etc., always gets on to me without any delay as other people are put off till I have finished; for instance Nita rang me up the same night she got up here when I was in Delhi; she asked to speak to the Military Secretary and was instantly put straight through to me, the theory being that if anything important is to be told to me by telephone, or if I have anything very urgent to say on the telephone, I shall always be given clear line.

Next to my room is my personal assistant in his office. There is a balcony running right round outside with a most glorious view right over the mountains; certainly I have got the most delightful office in the building. The Private Secretary is on the ground floor whereas I am on the first floor and therefore have a much better view. Of course so far I feel rather a fish out of water but these conditions are such that I shall very soon get quite accustomed to them I think!!

Nita tells me that altogether we have got twenty-four servants in our house including the men who push our rickshaw; some of these are provided by the Government here and they wear the scarlet uniform of the Viceroy. By the by I am a Lt. Col. now; I got a telegram yesterday.

Joan and Anne and Biddy come up to me on every possible occasion and call me Colonel but that is a jest which will get stale in time!

I am afraid your first Mail to us went down on the *Sussex*.

Your affectionate son

Ralph

*Nita to her sister*

April 28th, 1916                                    Viceregal Lodge, Simla

Darling Sissiekins,

We had such a jolly dinner at Government House last night, I enjoyed it so much. We were forty all told. We assembled in the drawing-room and then Their Excellencies, preceded by Capt. Holland Hibbert and Lord Errington, walked in and went round shaking hands with every one. How very low the women curtsey! Her Ex. has a separate presentation. We were all arranged with our partners so as His Ex. shook hands with the last lady he gave her his arm and walked off, followed by Her Ex. and all the rest of us coupled. Behind each chair stands a khitmagar in flaming red and as we enter they all salaam together. I had a most interesting man on my right, Sir Charles Cleveland, Head of the Police and Secret Service of India. He was so interesting that I never gave my attention to the man on my left until dessert! As we leave the dining-room each lady in turn stands out in the middle of the room and makes a sweeping curtsey to the ground to the Viceroy and then backs out of the room. Her Ex. does it first, followed by all her guests; it is a horrible ordeal, all the men are standing at their places round the table. I've not experienced anything like it since dancing class days! After dinner we sat and talked in the drawing-room until the men came in, then the doors were flung open and we younger people danced for about an hour and a half. Their Ex.s processed off upstairs; we all curtseyed again. I do hate curtseying to Her Ex. as I have to even when I go and have Browning lessons with her. The girls came to my tennis party last Wednesday and enjoyed it. I've another next Wednesday and don't know any of the people I've asked. It is rather fun wondering what is going to turn up, something like a sixpenny dip. Nearly every one up here is very interesting as they are all Civil or Military officials. So many wives have husbands shut up in Kut, I had one to tennis on Tuesday and another is coming to lunch on Sunday. It is so pathetic, they are so hopeful and so plucky and I try and cheer them up tho' I really know what the fate of Kut is to be. Ralph is in the know about everything that is going on and is to go on in Mesopotamia; he had two hours' talk alone with the Commander-in-Chief yesterday and gets all the despatches direct from the scene of operations. His work couldn't be more interesting or fascinating than it is now. He likes Beauchamp Duff immensely and all his staff.*

Love and hugs from

Mid

*Sir Charles Cleveland (1866–1929) was Director of Central Intelligence, India 1910–19.

The Browning Lessons were possibly on the poet Robert Browning.

The garrison at Kut al Amara, with a high proportion of Indian troops, held out for 143 days before surrendering to the Turks on 29 April, 1916. The Garrison Commander was Major-General Sir Charles Townshend.

General Sir Beauchamp Duff (1855–1918) was Commander-in-Chief India 1913–16. He had been Chief of Staff in India 1906–09.

*Nita to her family*

June 8th, 1916 Viceregal Lodge, Simla

Darling Family,

This has been a real black week, first the naval battle which was officially reported at first as a terrible disaster. We had lost fourteen ships to the Germans' three or four. Ralph got the first wire, it was not made public. About three days later better news arrived and it was published. The Viceroy is Chief Censor so we get very scrappy information as it is never thought advisable to let the truth be known to the Indians. We had only just got over it when Kitchener's death came upon us, the biggest bombshell of all. We were in bed when Pick brought up the letter containing the deciphered wire; it simply stunned us. Ralph dressed and rushed off to Viceregal Lodge and talked it over with HE; a second wire came in shortly after with the King's eulogy so they decided to make it public and

Ralph sent me a chit. I was downstairs with the working party for St
John. No one there knew but Joan and me so we wrote out a notice
and put it on a board for all the women to see; it was better than
telling them, it prevented the story from getting exaggerated in the
telling.*

Everything has been put off, the polo tournament and all the
dances which were taking place this week. The garden fête on
Saturday is to be held because St John Ambulance Assoc. will
suffer if it is cancelled. We are going to have a Memorial Service
the same day as in London but we have not heard yet when it is to
be. Pick is busy making me a black dress.

Nita

*The Battle of Jutland, 31 May, 1916, a success for the Germans in numerical
terms, but a strategic success for the British in that the High Seas Fleet never
again challenged British dominance of the North Sea.

Lord Kitchener was drowned when HMS *Hampshire* was sunk by a mine West of
the Orkneys on June 5th, 1916.

*Nita to her sister*

July 16th, 1916                          The Retreat, Mashobra

Darling Sissiekins,

We are still out here and loving it just as much. It is supposed to
be a rest cure for me but I have my peace invaded by some member
of the family or staff nearly every day. Margaret Abel-Smith calls
me Peacemaker to the Court as I seem to spend all my time settling
disputes, lecturing the Thesigers and giving advice all round.
There have been an awful lot of rows lately at V.L. over the girls'
bad manners and for weeks past I've listened to tales of complaint
from the staff, particularly about Joan. They all took a violent
dislike to her and she, feeling it, came to me and gave me the very
opening I wanted and I gave it to her hot. She was awfully nice,
very penitent and humble and acted on my advice straight away.
Miss Hogge, the governess, used to come and weep on my shoulder
about the waywardness of Biddy. She finally broke down and took
to bed and on getting up told Her Ex. what people and the staff in
particular thought of her family. Ralph was sent for to confirm it

and all three girls had bad half-hours with both parents and were then sent out here, Joan excepted, with Miss Hogge. I had a cheery weekend; Miss H. had hysterics before I got her to her bedroom and spent all her time chasing me into corners to pour out her woes. Bid sulked and Anne was rude to them both, both the girls kept me up to all hours and invaded my bedroom at dawn to give their versions. I lectured Biddy and reduced her to tears; there is no doubt she is getting very spoilt and abominably rude, especially to people outside V.L. She is a very dear impulsive warm-hearted girl and really quite my favourite. I listened to her point of view and rather sympathized, then put it before Miss Hogge when she was rather calmer because if Bid ever tried to give it herself she was told she was argumentative and impertinent.

The consequence of all this talky talky was that they all departed on Monday from here the best of friends, laughing and joking together and they have still kept it up. Miss Hogge was maudlingly grateful before she left. She got on my nerves from that Friday to Monday until I could have screamed; she pursued me in nightmares all night.

Biffy Holland-Hibbert came out to my rescue one Saturday for lunch; it was teeming cats and dogs but he rode the seven miles out most cheerfully. We escaped from the family for the whole afternoon. He also wants sympathy and help. He appears to be in love with several girls and does not know which he likes best!! He always looks very rosy and cherubic so never gets any sympathy for being ill. He is not at all strong and goes away and faints on his bed.

According to various reports, Ralph is a great success as Military Secretary, firstly because he is so very calm and never gets fussed over anything and because he is never influenced in giving a decision by the fact that it will affect his popularity. He has taken a very stern line with many of the English men in his employ, and the staff are quite devoted to him. He is very stern with the girls and will brook no nonsense from them; they are really rather frightened of him; he had Joan up the other day before her father because she gave an order to the Band without any authority from her father or Ralph. She promised some subaltern who is getting up a Revue that he could have *12 men* from the Band as an orchestra.

HE is awfully good, he upholds R's authority in everything. Ralph is responsible for his safety and whenever HE goes out detectives are hidden all over the place. I've seen them lots of times squatting behind bushes in the garden. HE knows nothing of it. He can never go out alone in case of anything happening; the other day he escaped and got such a wigging from Ralph when he got back!!! The staff were awfully tickled when that last group was taken. Ralph did not approve of HE's clothes and sent him back to change which he did like a lamb, Her Ex. warmly supporting Ralph.

Ever your loving

Mid

*Ralph to his mother*

July 28th, 1916                              Viceregal Lodge, Simla

My dearest Mother,

Next winter I am putting the married staff into bungalows instead of in tents which they been using for the last three winters.

Some Cavalry bungalows near the Lodge are vacant so I have taken them over and shall go and inspect them with my super-intendent of Viceregal Estates, gardener, etc. and see what has to be done to them in the way of small repairs, papering, etc. etc., also making gardens. By taking over these bungalows I save putting up about forty-five big tents and can use that space in the grounds for more flowers and garden.

Margaret Abel-Smith is staying here now as Sir George Barnes is away on tour. Our German, Mr Buchner, is going later on to the Maharajah of Scindra whom I really know quite well now as he has stayed here twice and I also met him in Bombay.*

Amongst other things Buchner did not much like in the terms of agreement with Scindia was that though he was given a house it was unfurnished. I saw Scindia about this yesterday morning and he told me that that was according to the rules of his State and that he could not alter it, to which I absolutely agreed but I said there was nothing in his State rules to prevent him giving Buchner a little present of Rs1,000 towards the expenses of the furnishing of his house!! He quite saw this, and agreed to do so!!!

I also got a present of a trap horse and harness out of him for Buchner as I pointed out that B's heart was too bad to allow him to walk much.

Scindra is a most generous little man and was quite charming about it so long as I do not break any of his State Commandments!

I have just this morning got the report in about that unfortunate troop train journey from Karachi to Lahore some three weeks ago when a good many men died on the journey from heat stroke. The mistake was really in ever sending them straight from home out to Sind desert at that time of year. Nita and I did it on April 3rd three years ago in a first-class carriage and it was bad enough then.

Your very affectionate

Ralph

*As Buchner was German, it was not considered suitable that he should continue working for the Government in India and Ralph suggested that the Maharajah of Scindra should employ him in future.

August 2nd, 1916            Viceregal Lodge, Simla

My dearest Mother,

The great Mahommedan feast of the year has been on for some weeks and it was over yesterday, and today we have therefore been having great holidays. The Mahommedan members of the Viceroy's bodyguard have just been here to pay their respects to me; in the course of their few remarks they said the Mahommedans all over India had been praying for two things during the last few weeks. One was for success of the British Arms in this War and the other was that I might soon be made Commander-in-Chief in India!!! I found it difficult to keep my face.

I am in the middle of all the details of our tour next December. For one part of the journey by river in Burma our party occupies no less than eight steamers; for another part the charge for one big steamer to take the whole party for five days is about £2,000! But I am trying to get this reduced or else make some other arrangements. But the total cost of the trip will be very big.

Your very affectionate

Ralph

*Nita to her sister*

August 4th, 1916                    Viceregal Lodge, Simla

Darling Sissiekins,

I lead a most amusing life these days.

PRIVATE

I am the confidante of most of the staff and of the girls and Margaret Abel-Smith; it's as good as a play, the excitement over this weekend party and the heart burnings – each has confided in me the particular man and girl they want and it's too awful, they never seem to like the right one. A wants B but B is bored by A and asks me to get C, C is equally bored by B and wants D who badly wants A. They nearly drive me mad; there are at least eight telephones in Viceregal Lodge in different rooms. Yesterday I tried in vain to do my housekeeping. Four times I had to listen to four plans suggested by four different people to suit their own wishes. Margaret Abel-Smith and I go ahead today with Psyche, that's all right; tomorrow Joan and twenty others join us and I have just had a note from another ADC to enlist my help and get Nancy Lees out for him; she is a dear little girl, sister of Sir Thomas Lees who was out in Sydney. My work is going to be cut out getting all these couples properly sorted and left in peace. Fred and Joan are both amazingly tactless and will push in where they are not wanted, so I foresee a jolly holiday for myself. I think I must have aged in appearance, they all look upon me as an ancient.*

Since I wrote this last sentence three of them have rung me up, Anne, Joan and Biffy. It has been fixed up: Nancy Lees is coming, and Mr Metcalfe, for breakfast tomorrow. He and Psyche are both devoted to Margaret. A Canadian called Orde is coming too; he and Joan will pair, Margaret and Psyche, Biffy and Nancy, while I do tactful chaperone.

Thank heaven Mrs Bob Stephens is quite close so I'll be able to go to her.

I'll let you know how it goes off.

Mid

*Sir Thomas Lees (1886–1915) 2nd Bart, had been ADC to Lord Chelmsford in New South Wales in 1912. He died of wounds received in action in the Dardanelles. His widow married Viscount Alanbrooke.

*Nita to Ralph's sister*

August 16th, 1916                               Viceregal Lodge, Simla

My dearest Gwen,

Capt. H. Hibbert is much loved by both children and so is Capt. Sykes; they often come down here to lunch and spend the rest of the afternoon in the nursery.

On Monday, Capt. H. Hibbert who is 6 ft. 4 in. allowed himself to be put to sleep on Nurse's bed; he was entirely covered up with the quilt eiderdown and when he was allowed to get up was given a breakfast of broken biscuits from a spoon and had his hair brushed and hands washed by them both. Do you wonder they love him?

Capt. Sykes prefers to steeplechase along the passages on the wooden horse on rails and as he leaps the step into the day nursery tumbles over backwards and groans on the floor; John shrieks with laughter and shouts for more. Joscelyne hides her head in the sofa and weeps; it is much too realistic for her, but John has got past that stage now . . .

*Ralph to his mother*

August 23rd, 1916                    .           Viceregal Lodge, Simla

My dearest Mother,

Tomorrow week I am going with Their Ex.s to stay with the Maharajah of Patiala at a place called Chail about 30 miles from here. Maffey and Holland Hibbert are the only others coming.

On the 12th we are having a parade here on the parade ground when the Viceroy is going to present about 200 decorations for good service in the war to Indian officers and men. I have been working pretty hard at our Burma tour. For two days, coming down the river from Myitkyina, we travel by seven small steamers, quite separate from each other. I have a steamer to myself with my European clerk, and Maffey has one too. We all join up at Bhamo again and go together on a large steamer from there to Prome, when we take the train again to Rangoon. From Bhamo to Prome will take us from the 12th to the 19th December.

Much love to you all,
Your very affectionate son,

Ralph

# CHAPTER THREE

In September the Viceroy visits the Maharajah of Patiala and then returns to Simla. The Commander-in-Chief India, Sir Beauchamp Duff, is recalled to London to face enquiries into the problems of Mesopotamia. Nita takes over as secretary of the Red Cross in Simla.

In October the Viceroy goes on a tour of Hardwar and Mohand and then back to Dehra Dun. In November he goes on a major tour to Agra, Jaipur and Udaipur, and then back to Delhi.

*Ralph to his mother*

September 3rd, 1916                    Viceroy's Camp, India, Chail

My dearest Mother,

We are staying here as the guests of the Maharajah of Patiala and this is his country house. A place about thirty miles by road from Simla but nothing more than six miles as the crow flies, and from my bedroom window I look right across to Viceregal Lodge and I can also just see Curzon House.

We came on here by motor and the last ten miles was absolutely glorious; a most lovely scene it is, and we were going along a narrow and very, very twisty road climbing up to this height from the river; we are higher here than Simla.

Their Ex.s, Fred and Holland Hibbert are in the Guest House, Maffey and myself in another house about ten minutes' walk distant. The Maharajah's Controller met us and had done everything he could for our comfort. We found on our dressing-tables in our bedrooms two bottles of scent each, hairwash from Paris, also a box of cigars and a box of cigarettes!!

Your very affectionate son

Ralph

*Nita to her mother*

September 8th, 1916                    Viceregal Lodge, Simla

Darling Mumpty,

I had a long talk with the poor little Commander-in-Chief [Sir Beauchamp Duff] after dinner. I feel so sorry for him, his career is at an end; as he told me last night Asquith wants his head on a charger, and to make a scapegoat of him for the Mesopotamia Campaign; he talked most bitterly about it and said he has a first rate case to lay before the English public but knows he will never be allowed to clear himself, that Asquith will say his statements cannot be made public for military reasons. He told me that was how the papers about Mesopotamia were treated when the Secretary of State was asked by the members of the House of Commons to lay them on the table. Duff himself knew the papers from beginning to end and said there was not a word in them which would be of value to the enemy, but Asquith seeing they would clear him and Lake and compromise his Gov. refused to allow them to be made public and made one of his usual plausible speeches.*

I felt so sorry for him as he has lost his best friend in K. [Kitchener] to whom he was devoted. He told me how intensely shy K. always was and how he couldn't bear officers who wouldn't stand up to him and contradict him if they held opposite views. He talked to me for about three-quarters of an hour mainly about K., himself and Mesopotamia. When I got him on to a lighter vein I chaffed him and asked him to be godfather to the fox-terrier puppy given to me last week by Lord Errington; he is to be called Duff. The General was very tickled tho' inclined to harp on the old subject that he hoped it would be a greater success than he was.

His only son was killed last year and his wife is separated from him. So life at present must look very bitter.

Much love,

Tum

*In November 1914, two days after declaring War on Turkey, England invaded Mesopotamia, today's Iraq, from India, to protect the Anglo-Persian oil interests and to secure the district round the head of the Persian Gulf from the Turks. In April 1915 the British Army under General Townshend advanced up the Tigris river as far as Kut with the idea of taking Baghdad, but after initial success the Army was hemmed in in Kut; the efforts to relieve it failed and in April 1916 the garrison of 9,000 British and Indian troops had to surrender and the total effort cost the British 24,000 casualties.

The Royal Commission set up to enquire into this disaster came to the conclusion that the campaign had been undertaken without adequate forethought or sufficient preparation.

Asquith (1852–1928) had been Prime Minister since 1908. On December 5th, 1916, he was forced out of office and Mr Lloyd George became Prime Minister.

Lt-Gen Sir Percy Lake (1855–1940) was then Commander of the Forces in Mesopotamia. He had been Chief of the General Staff in India 1912–15.

*Ralph to Nita*

October 21st, 1916                                      Dehra Dun

My own Darling,

We arrived here about 7 p.m. this evening after a hard but successful day at Hardwar. The journey from Simla was quite uneventful. We got to Hardwar at 10.30 and found Sir James Meston with other officials there to meet us.

We were first of all taken in another small train and trolleys to see the great works that were going on there in connection with a big dam; this was fairly interesting but somewhat technical. About 1,000 men have been working at this for about three years and certainly a wonderful amount has been accomplished.

We then went across the Ganges in boats to the other side where we found elephants waiting for us. We did about six miles on these elephants to the Gurukul which is a large college founded about fourteen years ago and which now has about 150 students ranging from six or eight years old to twenty-five. Once they enter the college they are not allowed to leave it till they have finished their time, the idea being to bring them up in true Hindi style and principle and that they must not be corrupted by meeting other people.

Every kind of subject is taught there including English, but all the teaching is carried on in Hindi; Chemistry, Philosophy, etc., as well as more ordinary subjects. When we arrived, there were triumphal arches and all the students lined the road dressed in yellow togas. The teachers and the principal were under the main gateway. We were all garlanded and proceeded in procession up the main drive and were shown over the many class-rooms where lessons where going on. We inspected dormitories, library, dining-room and then went onto the playground, where every kind of game was going on from Giant's Steps to Hockey. We ended up with very welcome refreshments of fruit and soda-water. All the students assembled at the Main Gate for our departure and HE made a short speech and gave them a whole holiday tomorrow in honour of his visit.

We mounted our elephants again, and after about a mile came to the lunch camp provided by Sir J. Meston; it was all very well done, and we stayed there after lunch for about half an hour before mounting our elephants again for the journey home. We had to cross the Ganges once again and had a cup of tea in a delightful bungalow on the banks of the river before going back to the station in motor-cars. The sun was pretty hot all day and we got through a good deal of sightseeing but I think we all enjoyed it very much and it was our first experience of a really Indian show, with the garlands and the elephants and the jungle.

Tomorrow we hope to play golf in the afternoon. I hope you enjoyed your tennis this afternoon. I shall probably get a letter from you tomorrow morning as the Mail comes in at 7.30 a.m.

Very much love my own darling,
Your very affectionate

Ralph

P.S. I forgot to tell you on our way back, when we crossed the river again after leaving our elephants, I tried going on a curious kind of boat which was really a charpoy or one of those Indian beds turned upside down and resting on two huge blown out skins of some animal rather larger than a big pig. Two boys, one on each of two other skins, lying on their tummies hung on to this strange craft and used their legs like small paddlewheels just to guide it; the stream carried us down. One cannot go against the stream so when they want to go up stream they deflate the skins and carry the whole thing back on their shoulders ready for another trip down stream again. I sat on this bed and held on to the legs; it was quite comfortable but one seemed to be very much at the mercy of the current; when we wanted to stop the boys guided us near to the bank where we grounded.

Ralph

October 23rd, 1916          Viceroy's Camp, Mohand

My own Darling

We came out to this camp leaving Dehra Dun after lunch this morning. Maffey and I played a round of golf on the links and enjoyed it immensely; I gave him a stroke a hole and I only just beat him.

This camp looks large enough to me to house a battalion; there are two bungalows in which Their Ex.s and the ladies live, including Mrs de Gale; the others are in tents near, but Maffey and I have two excellent tents some little way below, close to the river. I should think we must have nearly fifty tents pitched altogether and we have three motor-cars out here besides ponies, thirty cows, twelve elephants, though I have not yet seen the latter.

This is a most awfully pretty camp and I think we shall all enjoy it. Austen Smith has gone out riding my pony this evening to see if he likes it.

Austen Smith has just come back and says he likes the pony immensely and wants to buy him, so I shall be on the lookout for another one in Calcutta or Delhi. It was most awfully hot here today but I can see that the nights are going to be quite cold.

Well good night and God bless you and the children; I hope you did not over do it at your working party this morning.

Your own husband

Ralph

November 4th 1916                                Viceroy's Camp, Agra

My own Darling

Well we arrived here at 8.30 a.m. and the whole station was beautifully decorated with red carpets, flags, flowers, etc. etc. The first thing that happened was that, when I got out onto the platform and went up to meet Sir James Meston, the band of the Guard of Honour played the King, presented arms etc. while the Viceroy was still in his carriage, waiting for me to fetch him! He of course came out with a white face and for a moment very angry, but it was my fault and I chaffed him about it afterwards and he was quite all right. But I have wired to Jaipur strong orders to the effect that the National Anthem is NOT to be played until the Viceroy has actually stepped out, onto the platform from the train.

Everything else went off very well and we motored up to the circuit house for breakfast. There was a Guard of Honour there of the 24th Batn. Rifle Brigade. As a matter of fact there were only about five men in the whole regiment who used to belong to the regiment; the batn. is made up of men from nearly every regiment in the service, but the adjutant is a man called Plant who used to

be a corporal in the 2nd Batn.; I vaguely remember him and hope
to see him while I am here.

I have already discovered that it is the Military Secretary whom
everybody wants to see on this sort of show; the officer of the guard,
the policeman in charge of the sentries, the gardener in charge of
the garden, etc. etc., all come round to see the Military Secretary.
In fact I was hard at it from after breakfast till lunch. This is why I
do not feel I ought to be away from Gov. House, Calcutta, when we
go there; it is my job to be there and to be interviewed by all these
tiresome people!

Ralph

November 9th, 1916                    Viceroy's Camp, Jaipur

My own Darling

We have had a most wonderfully interesting day and I wish you
could have seen it. We got to the station at 8.30 a.m. and found all
the officials on the platform and also the Maharajah of Jaipur.
When Their Ex.s got out of the train the Guard of Honour of his
State troops and the band played a tune which was supposed to be
the National Anthem. The Viceroy inspected the Guard of Honour
but they were a very dirty and slovenly looking crowd; I went in the
front of the first car with the Maharajah and the Viceroy in the back
of it. All the streets were lined with his troops. When we started
off more bands made more noises. One lot of soldiers we passed
were all armed with very supple swords; they leaned forward and
shouted and waved these swords at us in the most threatening
looking manner; this was their form of saluting.

We passed elephants most beautifully painted and dressed up in
gorgeous-looking trappings, also little cannons in tiny little carriages
drawn by bullocks, every kind of uniform you can imagine, some very
splendid and others very much the reverse. Every band we passed
made noises with drums and awful sounding trumpets making no
particular tune but a man simply blew through it as hard as he
could.

We arrived at this Residency which certainly is magnificent. Mrs
Benn the wife of the resident was waiting at the top of the steps for
HE, a splendid shamiana was erected, red and gold carpet, etc.
Our first ceremony after arrival was the deposition of four sirdars

who were received by Wood and myself and came to enquire after
HE's health; after a few minutes' talk we gave them attar and pan;
the former is sprinkled on their handkerchiefs and the latter is
wrapped up in palm leaves and just put into their hands.*

We then had breakfast. At 10.30 a.m. we left by special train to
go three miles away where the Viceroy opened a new railway in the
presence of the chief sirdars and the Maharajah, etc. Before lunch
there was an exhibition of the most wonderful things made in
Jaipur. I only bought two little brass things for the children, but if
you had been with me I am sure I would have bought any amount:
brass bowls, wonderful embroidery, daggers, etc.

After lunch came the official visit of the Maharajah to the Viceroy.
He arrived in a most wonderful carriage drawn by four horses with
about fifty scarlet men running and shouting in front. He was
received in the shamiana, all the Viceroy's staff and the residents
in full dress, white uniform on one side and the Maharajah's sirdars
on the other; they both sat on two gold thrones and talked, Col.
Benn being interpreter. Attar and pan was given by the Viceroy to
the Maharajah and then by Wood to all his sirdars. After about a
quarter of an hour they all left and at 3.45 p.m. we started off in
motors to return the call at his palace in the centre of the city.

This was the most wonderful thing I have ever seen; we arrived at
the big gate of the palace in the motors and from there up to the
inner courtyard, the road was lined by his extraordinary troops
who made frightful noises on all the bands, blowing the trumpets,
beating the drums, etc. When the Viceroy got out of the motor he
was put into a silver palanquin and carried shoulder high by about
twenty men, all of us walking on either side of him, through more
troops, up to the big flight of steps leading to the Durbar Hall
where were assembled about 1,000 Jaipur celebrities in the most
wonderful clothes you ever saw.

We processed up the centre of the Durbar Hall to the two thrones
which were on a gold raised dais. All these nobles were dressed in
wonderful silks with priceless jewels, but their lower garment was a
white petticoat with dozens of folds; it looked most peculiar.

After HE and the Maharajah had talked for a little the Band of
Nautch Girls came in and danced in front of the Viceroy to the
music of the Jaipur instruments and drums or rather tomtoms. This
was not very exciting, but still the whole scene was just like a huge

show at Olympia. The ceremony of the attar and the pan was gone through again but the other way round; the Maharajah presented them to the Viceroy after putting a garland round his neck, his Prime Minister did the same for all of us. We went through exactly the same procession on leaving the Durbar. Her Ex. and the ladies of the party were up in the gallery behind us, so saw it all from there.

I simply cannot describe to you the wonderful effect of colour this Durbar had as we approached it, with the Viceroy being carried in this huge palanquin. It was far finer than any show I have ever seen at any theatre in London, and the Maharajah had certainly taken immense trouble to make a good show because the Viceroy had consented to return his visit in his own palace.

Very much love, Your own husband

Ralph

*In *Hobson-Jobson*, Yule and Burnell's *Glossary of Colloquial Anglo-Indian Words and Phrases*, Shameeane (sic) is described as an awning of flat tent-roof, sometimes without sides . . . pitched like a porch before a large tent; often used by civil officers, when on tour, to hold their court of office proceedings in a manner generally accessible.
  Attar: a fragrant essence obtained from rose petals.
  Pan: a combination of betel leaf, areca nut and lime used as a masticatory.
  Sirdars: Indian Officers.


November 11th, 1916                          Viceroy's Camp, Jaipur

My own Darling

Our visit to Tonk went off all right, but it has been a long and rather dull day. It was sixty miles there but we did it in under the two hours; the road was lined with either soldiers or police the whole way, and it had been watered so there was no dust. The Resident there is a Mr Waterfield, whose wife died last year, but he went home and brought out another one with him last April.

The Nawab of Tonk is a fine old man of seventy-three though he looks much younger. He has had many domestic troubles lately. He married the other day a girl of seventeen, but a few days after the ceremony when we came up and he was in the full enjoyment of his connubial happiness, one of his sons came to him and told him that he could not really marry the girl because she had already been

married to himself. The case came up before Sir Elliot Colvin to
decide and he discovered that whatever else the son may have done
to the girl he had not married her, so she now remains with the old
Nawab and the son who had the audacity to claim her has been
banished for life from the State of Tonk!!*

The present old Maharajah of Jaipur is still going very strong in
that line and the population of Jaipur is still reputably increasing
thanks to the personal excellence of its ruler!!

Your own husband

Ralph

*Sir Elliot Colvin (1861–1914) had spent his life in the Indian Civil Service. From
1905 to 1917 he was Agent to the Governor-General in Rajputana.

November 13th, 1916                    Viceroy's Camp, Udaipur

My own Darling

Our arrival here was not nearly so impressive as at Jaipur
although the actual procession was more so because we were in
carriages with quite a smart escort, but there were not nearly so
many troops on the road. There were about six most magnificent
elephants dressed in gold and painted in many colours, but the
whole effect was nothing like so good.

Our visit to Chitor was quite interesting; it is a wonderful old
place but as you will see it for yourself, I need not describe it now.
There are two towers which I climbed up; if you go up one of them
be very careful because the steps are very steep and there are many
places where you can give your head a nasty knock; I think it is
worth your while your going up the taller of the two towers, though
as it stands on a lower level the top is not so high as the other one,
but the carving is better. But you will have to be very careful as you
might easily have a nasty fall as well as a nasty knock.

The Maharajah is a fine looking old man but not so cheery as
Jaipur who is a delightful old boy and still very naughty! This man
is said to have lived a blameless life and to have been wonderfully
faithful to his wife. He speaks no English. Wood and I had the
usual Mizaj Pursi ceremony at 6 p.m. when the four principal

sirdars came to enquire after the Viceroy's health, but their clothes were not nearly so gorgeous as Jaipur's.

Your own husband,
Ralph

November 23rd, 1916            Viceregal Lodge, Delhi

My own Darling

There has been a proper row about Biddy and Metcalfe. Miss Hogge went to Her Ex. and said she would not stand his attentions to Biddy any longer; he also got to hear that she had done so and went up to her and abused her pretty strongly which did not help matters, then Miss Hogge got hold of me and poured out her views and asked me to help matters immediately after that. As I was on my way to my office, Metcalfe came out and asked to speak to me and gave me his story and asked me to go to Her Ex. for him. Her Ex. had meanwhile told the Viceroy who was white with rage and told Maffey that Metcalfe had better go at once if he could not behave like a gentleman. Then finally Maffey came to see me and asked me to go up to the house and calm down the family!! So I had my hands pretty full yesterday afternoon. I am glad to say everybody is better this morning. I have got Her Ex. into a good mood and she is going to see Metcalfe quite in a friendly way. Biddy has had more than one interview with her mother who has rather told her not to be silly and that she must consider herself still in the schoolroom, and that her first job must be her lessons. I got Her Ex. to say that probably Miss Hogge had taken a very exaggerated view of the whole thing, but she would not allow that Miss Hogge gives Biddy a bad time and says that even if Biddy does not care for her very much, she has to stick to her and not take up the attitude of being given a bad time of it, or else she shall go straight back to school.*

Very much love, Your own
Ralph

*Aubrey Metcalfe (1883–1957) was Assistant Private Secretary to the Viceroy 1914–17. He was educated at Charterhouse and Christ Church, Oxford, so he should have known how to behave like a gentleman. He was created KCIE in 1936.

# CHAPTER FOUR

In December the Viceroy goes on another major tour to Allahabad, Calcutta, Rangoon, Bhamo, down the Irrawaddy, Manda Day then back to Calcutta and Barrackpore and Dehli.

In April the Viceroy visits the Khyber Pass and inspects 900 retired Indian Army Officers. Then to Lahore where he holds a Durbar, then back to Dehra Dun via Amritsar.

December 2nd, 1916                    Government House, Rangoon

My own Darling,

We had a most wonderful arrival here yesterday. At 7.45 a.m. I went on the wharf to receive the Lt. Governor and brought him on board where he met Their Ex.s. We landed at 8 a.m. in procession, with mace bearers and all the staff two and two walking in front of them, Maffey and I coming immediately behind them. The whole place was smothered in flags and on the quay there was a huge pandal or reception tent erected which was supposed to hold 1,200 people, in which the address was presented to him with a wonderful casket with a carved elephant tusk on top.

We then got into carriages and proceeded at a walking pace along crowded streets, everybody cheering like mad; it was most imposing. At each triumphal arch we came to, and there were no less than fifteen of these most beautifully decorated, HE received an address in some sort of silver casket and also a bouquet; the carriage was simply packed with these things. We arrived here and who do you think was commanding the Guard of Honour of the Rangoon volunteers? Mr Henstock!! The last time I saw him was when he waved goodbye to us from the gardener's cottage at Plas! I was not able to talk to him then but I saw both him and his wife at the races on the lake yesterday afternoon; they are both very well and she looked very cheery and bright.[1]

The boat races on the lake were quite lovely. When we first arrived there was an open air theatre with a Burmese troupe with the leading actor who is very well known in Burma. He is said to be so terribly attractive to the Burmese ladies that he has to have police protection wherever he goes! I am told he is very faithful to his Burmese wife so I am afraid he does not make the most of his opportunities!! They did a sort of dance to a Burmese band and it was quite amusing.

After tea we all went on the state barge pulled along by about six canoes, the crews of which were dressed in different colours; blue, pink etc., one canoe having the Burmese band on it. The banks were crammed with a wonderfully picturesque crowd dressed in all the colours of the rainbow. We went a round on the lake at a very slow and stately pace and then returned to the golden platform and canopy under which we had more tea.

After we had returned to Government House I went off with Sir Harcourt Butler for a drive in the motor. I had a most splitting headache and felt most frightfully ill; Maffey was also very seedy. I was rather sick before dinner but struggled down because I thought it would upset the arrangement of the table. I took one of the Aspirin tablets you gave me and had absolutely nothing to eat at all, all through dinner, but kept sipping champagne. I was sitting next to a very pretty girl, a Mrs Foster, and that revived me by degrees until at the end of dinner I was able to put up quite a respectable flirtation with her!! She asked me if I was wearing these pretty blue facings to my coat because I was an ADC!! So I said that all the staff wore them, so she asked what I was on the staff. When I told her I was Military Secretary she apologised for not knowing but said I was much too young looking to be a colonel; so you see we got on all right![2]

This morning we started off at 6.45 a.m. to see the Rangoon River works and the timber yards where the elephants pull and push and lift these huge logs of timber. I have seen it before when I was here in 1907, but it was very interesting. On the steamer we had breakfast and you never saw such a meal; the coffee cups were about the size of thimbles and the menu was chiefly composed of cold beef, cheese, etc. though I confess I did get a bit of an omelette. They kept pressing us to take liqueurs of every colour and whiskey and soda was the principal drink. The waiters were too few and did nothing but take our plates away without bringing us anything to eat. Biffy got the giggles and it really was a comic meal. I was sorry for the Chairman of the River Board, a funny little man who kept jumping up from his chair next to HE in order to go and damn the caterer!! I was not feeling at all strong myself but I could not help being amused at it; this meal must have taken at least three quarters of an hour to serve. I never saw such a poor attempt at breakfast, but as a comic item on the programme it was a huge success.

This Government House is a most sumptuous place, our bedrooms are magnificent and each bedroom has its own bathroom; they were copied from the Carlton Hotel at home. There is a huge drawing-room with a very much carved ceiling, supported by white pillars. It is really wonderfully cool here, much cooler than I expected, but anyhow this house has got so many fans that one could keep cool in much greater heat than this. I am always wishing you were here to see this place and I must try and bring you here some day.

You never saw such wonderful presents as the Viceroy has had in the way of caskets, they must be worth hundreds of pounds. I am having them all put out for him to see; most of them are in great cases standing three feet high; models of boats, of houses, of elephants, etc. etc., all in Burmese silver. I do not know what he will do with them all when he gets back to 18 Queen's Gate Place.

I shall think of you arriving in Delhi tomorrow night and do hope you're keeping well; I am practically all right again now.

Very much love my own dearest heart. Your own husband

Ralph

[1]Plas is a Verney home in Anglesey.
[2]Sir Harcourt Butler (1869–1938) was Lt-Governor of Burma 1915–17; Governor of Burma 1923–27.

December 4th, 1916                    Government House, Rangoon

My own Darling,

We are having a glorious time of it here. Yesterday after church we had a private view of the Arts and Crafts Exhibition and it really was very well worth seeing – inside were all the finished articles of every description and outside were booths and tents in which all the various trades were being carried on; little Burmese girls painting the tops of parasols, men doing carving in wood and ivory and silver, a large rubber exhibit, candle and match making, etc. etc. I bought a good deal including a long piece of Burmese silk for a dress for you. All these things will be sent here after the exhibition is over and they will be packed up and sent straight onboard the *Rankola* for us. I also bought two carpets made in the jail here, and a nice basket-work table. The carpets wash very well and will do excellently for the veranda or the lawn; also a laquer bowl, a tray and a small gong such as is carried by the pack bullocks in Burma, which I think you will like. I did not care very much for the carved silver things here nor did I see any very good wood carving, but I shall look out for one or two more things in Mandalay and will get you a Burmese god if I see a good one.

This afternoon we have had a big garden party here which was a delightful show because of the many bright coloured clothes worn by the Burmese men and women. There was also a troupe of Burmese girl dancers with a Burmese band and a juggler; there were said to be nearly 3,000 people at it. Anne was seedy so did not appear.

This morning we started off at 7 a.m. and went all over an oil refinery which was very interesting. I had no idea how many things were made out of oil, such as candles. We had what were called light refreshments in the middle; these consisted of caviar sandwiches chiefly, which were excellent. We had not had any breakfast, so tucked into these without any serious results so far. We got back at 11 a.m. and had a proper breakfast then and at 12 o'clock Their Ex.s performed the opening ceremony of this Arts and Crafts Exhibition. After Their Ex.s had gone, I stayed behind with Sir Harcourt and went all over it again but did not buy anything more.

Your own husband

Ralph

December 11th, 1916                              Steamer *Taping*
                                                Irrawaddy, Burma

My own Darling,

We changed into this steamer yesterday at Bhamo and I think we are all sorry to leave our smaller steamers which were very peaceful and comfortable. Their Ex.s and Anne are on a barge tied alongside but there is a gangway connecting the two, and we go on board their barge for meals.

We went on shore yesterday afternoon and had the usual sort of show with Burmese dances and presents from a few chiefs, and a large crowd of school children, etc. The Deputy Commissioner who ran the show was a most popular man called Lewison whose father was a German. I could not help thinking he had had one or two drinks to steady his nerves before the Viceroy's arrival; he was very fussy and kept making various signals for people to do different

David Verney, the Editor. See p. 108: The baby as as ugly as it could be but there was hope of its nproving in looks.

10. Nita's Kitmagar (centre) with domestic staff at Simla

11. Nita with John (left), David (centre) and Jocelyn in Delhi, about 1920

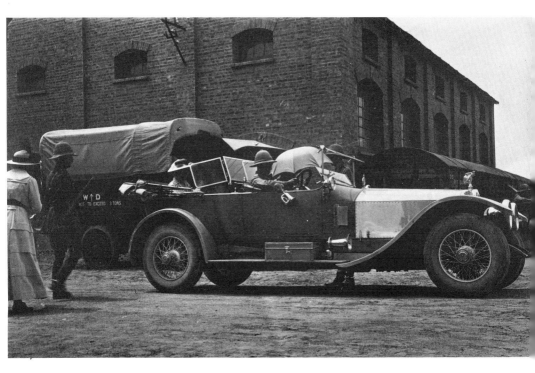

12. Transport: Viceregal Rolls Royce

13. Mail phaeton

14. Ralph and Nita on elephant

15. Nita and camel

16. Travel by rickshaw

17. Lady Chelmsford sketching; a 'typical stud[...]
See p. 143

18. Aubrey Metcalfe, Joan Thesiger, Sykes, Nita

19. Sightseeing at Amber, left to right, (Europeans): Col. A. Smith,
    Anne, Hawkey, Joan Thesiger, Mr J.L. Maffey, Ralph, Capt. Wilfrid
    (Biffy) Holland-Hibbert, H.E., Col. Benn

20. At the Kutub: Nell Anderson, Nita, Major Alexander, Ralph

21. H.E. with family and European staff. Back row: Major J. Mackenzie, Comptroller; H.A. Metcalfe, APSV; Capt. C. Sykes, ADC; Capt. W.A. Brown, ADC; Major Cotterill, Surgeon; W. Holland-Hibbert, ADC; Mr Maffey, PSV; Ralph Verney, MSV; Capt. Lord Errington, ADC. Front row: Hon. Bridget Thesiger, Hon. Anne Thesiger, Hon. Margaret Thesiger, Her Ex., H.E., Hon. Joan Thesiger, Miss Hogge

22. Arriving at Jaipur Railway Station, 1916. Left to right: Capt. Brown, Ralph, W. Holland-Hibbert, Her E., H.H. The Maharajah. See p. 42

23. Viceroy's camp at Jaipur

24. With the Maharajah of Jaipur and his son, left to right: Miss Knox, Ralph and Nita. See p. 59

25. The Golden Temple, destroyed by riote in the 1980s at Amritsar, the scene of riots 1919. See p. 63

26. Island on which the English took refuge in the Mutiny

things such as waving his handkerchief violently for the school children to cheer, beckoning all and sundry to come here or go there and then, when he was presenting the native chiefs to Their Ex.s in a big kind of Pandal, he lent up against a post and tried to make rather feeble jokes about them as they came up and kept saying 'all is quite unrehearsed on their part, they are doing it quite of their own free will, no compulsion of any kind'. But his greatest effort was bringing up to Sheepshanks some bills for supplies which he had been asked to get and have put onboard here. Among these was an item for eight ox tails; apparently they were not procureable so instead of cutting that item out he bought eight oxen, had them killed, gave us the eight ox tails and charged us 300 Rs. for them! Fancy 300 Rs. for eight ox tails! He then told Sheepshanks that the bills must all be paid before we sailed from Bhamo. Then we ordered fifteen seers of fresh milk; for this same amount at Myitkyina, which was a much smaller place, we paid 2 Rs. 9 annas; his bill came to 94 Rs.!! because he thought ordinary cows were not good enough, so he had hired cows for the last three weeks and charged us for the food of the cows, the hire of a man to look after them, etc. etc. Another item was for 116 Rs. for vegetables; this was all right but he charged 121 Rs. for wages and the expenses of the man who brought them from Myitkyina, giving him allowances of about £1 a day. Sheepshanks gave me these bills to deal with and I took them straight off to Sir Harcourt Butler who said he would settle the matter with the chief commissioner of the district. I met our friend Lewison this morning before we started, and so I said to him, as regards the bills he wanted paid before we started, I had given them over to the Lt. Governor from whom he would hear in due course; the only thing he said was, 'Oh Lord!!'*

I am told he has the reputation of being a clever man but I thought him either drunk or dotty, and I was most certainly not going to have the Viceroy stung to that extent. To add to the joke about his charge for the fresh milk, when we arrived Their Ex.s were given tinned milk for their tea!!

We had a very pretty journey indeed this morning through a defile, but yesterday's trip from up the river to Bhamo was absolutely gorgeous through a very narrow defile in which the water in the river was all whirlpools; when the river is in flood the water rises no less than 120 feet. I went up onto the roof of my little steamer and sat there for over two hours with a topee and dark glasses on, and enjoyed the scenery wishing you were there with me; you would have loved it.

Last night when it got dark there were 10,000 little floating lamps – made of paper and bamboo and a candle – coming down the river from about a mile or so higher up; they were different colours and were quite lovely and went on for hours, it was one of the prettiest things we have seen.

Your own husband

Ralph

*Seer: An Indian denomination of weight, varying widely in different parts of the sub-continent.

*Ralph to his Mother*

December 13th, 1916                    Viceroy's Camp, Burma

My dearest Mother,

We're now on our way down the Irrawaddy; we came on small steamers from Myitkyina right up in the north near the Chinese frontier to a place called Bhamo; when we got there we were transferred into this big boat, Their Ex.s and Anne being on a barge which is tied alongside with a gangway between.

At each place we got to we were met by lots of racing canoes paddled by about thirty to forty natives, one native standing up in the middle clanging a gong to keep the rowers in time, and usually two or three others, standing in the middle of the canoe, playing Burmese instruments. Another man standing up near the bow is usually doing a Burmese dance which consists, for the most part, in swinging his arms about and swaying his body in time to the music.

A Burmese crowd is most picturesque because of the bright clothes they wear; all these clothes were reflected in the waves, and the sun was shining, and the whole scene was quite lovely.

We are on this boat for no less than nine days, tying up every night, and most days stopping at some place or other to see oil fields or have a small reception.

I think the most lovely sight we have yet seen was the boat races on the big moat at Mandalay. The old palace there with its grounds is on a big square piece of 1¼ miles each side; a huge moat was made all round so that the moat is 5 miles long altogether, and is about 80 yards wide. The present Government House is built on one of the old gates of this palace and so looks right over this moat; the races were held just in front and on the opposite bank were thousands of Burmese in their gay clothes, with equally gay cloth parasols, all reflected in the water of this moat.

Many of the crews paddle their canoe standing up on one leg, using the other leg to help push the paddle through the water; they hold on to a rail with one hand so that they paddle with one hand and one leg. There were several crews of women who always do it this way. The canoes are very long and very narrow. Then they have a peculiar mode of deciding the winner of a race; instead of the ordinary winning post they have a bamboo upright with a bamboo cross-piece about 2 ft. from the water; in this hollow cross-piece is a cane sticking out about 2 or 3 ft. each end. One boat has to go to one side of this, and the other boat the other side. The leading man in the canoe has to pull out the cane from the bamboo and whoever gets the cane wins the race, so that there can be no doubt at all as to who is the winner, and the man steering the canoe has to bring his boat just so that the man in the bows can reach the cane and never miss it. When it is a very near thing the man in the middle urges the rowers on to further effort by clanging his gong louder and quicker than ever. It is a most curious thing to watch.

Very much love,<br>
Your very affectionate

Ralph

28th December, 1916                                  Viceroy's Camp, India
                                                              Barrackpore

My dearest Mother,

We came out here from Calcutta yesterday, though I myself could only get here today as this morning I had a rehearsal of the big Proclamation Parade which is being held on January 1st in Calcutta, which the Viceroy is to attend; all the troops were out on parade and I rode the Viceroy's charger and took his place riding round the troops, after which they all marched past me. It was rather fun.

Our public arrival in Calcutta went off very well indeed and was most impressive. We all wore our full dress uniform for the first time. It was all photographed on the cinema; and at Government House, after dinner one night, we had a private view of this film which was most amusing. Nita was at Gov. House and I just caught sight of her in an upper window while I was going around the Guard of Honour. The Viceroy has had a most awfully busy time since we arrived.

The first morning he received no less than eleven different deputations from high-ranking officials in Calcutta. Each deputation presented an address and each had to receive a separate reply, many of them requiring quite lengthy speeches. I am glad to say that the preparation of these speeches is done in the private secretary's department, and I have only to be responsible for the reception of the deputations, and the seating of them, etc.

Then another morning from 10 until 1.30 we were paying official calls on India chiefs; each chief first calls on the Viceroy and then about an hour later he goes and returns it. It's an awful waste of time but, of course, the chiefs think a great deal of being allowed to pay these official calls; guns saluting them, whether coming or going, were firing away all the morning. The Viceroy has thirty-one guns as his salute and most of the chiefs thirteen or fifteen each.

Your very affectionate

Ralph


January 25th, 1917                          Viceregal Lodge, Delhi

My dearest Mother,

On February 2nd I am going with the Viceroy to stay the weekend with the Maharajah of Dholpur, returning early Monday morning. About the 8th March I much hope to be able to get away, from a Wednesday to a Monday, with Maffey to Jaipur.

On March 26th we go off on tour again to Gwalior. Her Ex. is not coming for this trip as it will be very hot, but she will join us in Lahore on April 5th when they are planning an official visit there, and after that we go on to Peshawar for a week before returning to

Simla about April 17th. That is our rough programme for the spring.

Very much love,

Your very affectionate

Ralph

5th February, 1917                  Viceregal Lodge, Delhi

My dearest Mother,

I got back this morning from a visit to the Rana of Dholpur with the Viceroy. The Rana took us all over the place in a beautiful Rolls Royce, but I have never been over such rough country in a motor before, not even in Australia. He has tracks made across country for motoring, but the only thing that is seen is that the stones are moved away and placed along each side just to mark out the track. On our way back on the Saturday evening we passed a small herd of Nilgai. A Nilgai is an animal about the size of a cow.

For the trip to Dholpur, I wrote to the Rana to ask him to ask the Viceroy and when the invitation came I took it to HE and told him he must accept it!! He vastly enjoyed it and the weekend away did him a lot of good. He kept asking me on Sunday evening if I had not had any telegrams to show him from Mesopotamia, etc. I could truthfully say I had not had any; this however was not surprising in view of the careful instructions I had given before leaving Delhi that none were to be forwarded!! Luckily, on my return home, I found there was nothing that mattered waiting till today. So all is well.

We had a most successful parade here last week for the Viceroy to give some War decorations. We headed the list of 200 with three VCs which caused endless enthusiasm. We had about 600 spectators and a Guard of Honour of about 200 men, besides our bodyguard of 50 men strong.

Your very affectionate

Ralph

March 12th, 1917                              Viceregal Lodge, Delhi

My dearest Mother,

We came back yesterday from this place called Siwaimadophur which is in the State of Jaipur.

First of all I must tell you of the tragedy in the Maffey family. Their youngest baby, a girl of eleven months only, became very ill with some sort of poison on Wednesday afternoon and died the following morning. It is really terribly sad, and both of them are terribly cut up about it. I do not think anyone knows what caused it. It might have been just an ordinary fly which carried the poison.

Maffey had been prevented coming with us owing to some important work, but of course he would have had to cancel it anyway. Everything possible was done for the poor little thing and Col. Austen Smith [the Viceroy's surgeon] was with her all night long, fighting for her life. It must have been some poison which got into her milk. She was a very fat baby, and the doctor seemed to think her almost too fat. Everything in this country is so terribly sudden. She was perfectly well one afternoon, and then not only dead but buried the following afternoon.

Maffey was with the Viceroy at 4 p.m. and on getting back to his office found a telephone message from his wife telling him to come home at once. It has really cast such gloom over us all and indeed leaves one with such an uncomfortable feeling of insecurity. It would have been so dreadful if this had happened while the Maffeys were away with us at Jaipur, though of course he had already been stopped coming with us.

Well I must go on to the more cheerful news of our shoot. As the Maffeys could not come we took Capt. Holland Hibbert and Miss Knox. It was a great piece of luck for the latter coming for this experience just before going back to Australia, which she does this week. We left here by a special train provided for us by the Maharajah at 10 p.m. on Wednesday night and we arrived at Sawaimadopur early next morning and got out of the train at 7 a.m. Biffy (Capt. H.H.) and I went off shooting at 7.30 after partridges but without much success. We came back for breakfast in the Maharajah's guest house where we were staying and we heard that a tiger had eaten one of the kills during the night. A 'kill' is a buffalo tied up somewhere in the jungle as a bait for the tiger. If the tiger takes the kill there are men watching to see to which part of the jungle he goes. We started out the first day about 1 p.m., all the beaters having gone on ahead. There were about 1,500 of these beaters. We started off by motor along a very rough road for about two miles, then we got on elephants which took us right up to our machan, which was a very big one and could accommodate all of us four and also the old Maharajah and his little son of about ten. However, we had no luck that day as the tiger broke back and got out of the beat through the beaters. When after a tiger one must not shoot at anything else which comes out first because the great thing is to get the tiger and a shot would frighten him away.

We saw a black bear which we were not able to shoot at for this reason. However, after the beat was over and we knew the tiger had got away we had another small beat for this black bear and Biffy shot him after I had missed him.

On the second day we started off about the same time, but again the tiger broke back through the beaters and got away. But one of the shikaris, or men who are like keepers in England, came and told us this, so when a black bear came along I was able to shoot him, also a samba which is a kind of stag. So I got a samba and a black bear on the second day. Biffy was in another machan with Miss Knox, and he did not get a shot in at all.

The third day was our triumphal day when I got my first tiger. Curiously enough it was the second anniversary of the day I was wounded and also I shot him almost exactly at the same moment as I was hit, allowing for the difference in time. We heard again that a tiger had taken a kill but in a different part of the country. We only had about a mile to go in the motor then about another mile on elephants to our machan which was a big one. I had the best place, Biffy on my left. Nita stood just beside me. We were up in that machan quite an hour before the beat started as the men had a long way to go. One cannot mistake when the beaters begin because they make a tremendous noise, shouting, beating drums and yelling at the top of their voices in order to frighten the tiger away. Suddenly the Maharajah's private secretary who was with us spotted the tiger creeping along the side of a very steep rocky hill in front of us. Our machan was built on the side of this very steep ridge and men were posted on the top of it in order to drive the tiger down towards our machan after he tried to keep out of our reach. These men saw him creeping along and gave a shout which made him give two roars. I could not see him at all though I tried very hard and Nita saw him quite plainly about 300 yards away. He then disappeared in the thick undergrowth and we saw nothing of him for half an hour.

When the beat came a little nearer he suddenly came out of the thick scrub onto a clear place about eighty yards in front of us. He looked magnificent standing there staring straight at us. I fired but only hit him in the foot; he charged straight at us and I then killed him stone dead with a bullet through his neck. We had not expected anything else to come out but two samba came, both of which we got and then a panther came which Biffy hit with his first shot, missed with his second: I fired, missed my first shot but killed him with my second.

It is most unusual to get any other animals after there is a tiger about, because they all run away from him, but out of this one beat we got one tiger, one panther and two samba. Our total bag for the three days was a tiger, a panther, 2 black bears, 3 samba besides about 150 sand grouse which we shot before breakfast on the third morning. The excitement of all the natives when a tiger is killed is enormous: they all shout at the top of their voices and everybody goes mad with delight.

We were photographed on the spot with the tiger and then when it arrived back at the house we had another done by the Maharajah's official photographer so I hope to be able to send you a copy.

Certainly it was a wonderful three day's shoot and I much doubt if I shall have such an experience again during my time in India though I daresay I shall be at many more tiger shoots; but they will be given for the Viceroy and not for me, which makes the whole difference.

The Maharajah had a special carriage put on the train coming back for our benefit. The whole trip never cost us a penny from the time of leaving Delhi till we got back. Nita most really enjoyed it all and loved the life, riding in the early morning and then those shoots all day with elephants, etc.

I found a good lot of work waiting for me on my return which will take me a few days to get through but it is well worth it.

Your very affectionate son

Ralph

April 10th, 1917                    Government House, Peshawar

My own Darling,

We have just got back from our visit to the Mohmand Border. It was very interesting: we saw blockhouses and a live wire fence, also armoured cars in action. They put out some targets and three cars attacked these, firing as they advanced and retired. The General got a little nervous because he said in return for all this firing in Mohmand country we might possibly get a sniper firing back at us, so he moved us on fairly quickly and nothing exciting happened, but I got a message from him just before we left there suggesting that we should take off our black mourning bands from our arms [in memory of General Kitchener] in case they should be a mark for a sniper! I'm afraid I took no notice of this ridiculous suggestion!!

We had tea in one of the forts, and then got back home about 6 p.m. I found Molly here with Joan. She sends you her love. I think all this visit has been a very great success. We are looking forward to tomorrow's visit to the Malakand.

Your own

Ralph

April 13th, 1917                         Viceroy's Camp, India

My own Darling,

This morning we had a very good show out at the Cantonments; about 900 retired Indian Officers of whom quite six were old mutiny volunteers. After going round the whole lot which took us nearly $1\frac{1}{4}$ hours, HE came back to the central Flag Staff, a bugle sounded the Assembly and all those old boys raced across the ground to get the best place near HE to hear his speech. This was quite unrehearsed and was such a moving sight. HE read out his speech, and then he said a few words extemporare and said them in quite his most charming manner: how he had the honour of being the son of a soldier, and how immensely proud he was to have had the pleasure of meeting such a fine body of heroes who had done their best in the past for their King and Country, etc.

General Hudson then read out a translation of his written speech and there was quite an *uproar* of cheering when HE left. He was in frock-coat and star and looked the part splendidly.*

Yours ever,

Ralph

*General Sir Havelock Hudson (1862–1944) was Adjutant-General, India 1917–20. He later (1920–24) became GOC-in-C Eastern Army in India.

April 14th, 1917                                   Viceroy's Camp, India
                                                              Lahore

My own Darling,

I went out yesterday afternoon to fix up about the Durbar. It was to have been held in an old courtyard which was all covered in with huge awnings; the wind last night tore them to ribbons, blew down the poles and played havoc all round. So we have had to postpone the Durbar until Monday morning and shall have to hold it in the University Hall where we had the Convocation yesterday afternoon. His Ex. was given the Degree of Doctor of Laws by the University and was clothed in a huge scarlet gown of ample proportions. It was an imposing thing and he looked very well in it.

After that ceremony came four addresses from four communities each long, boring things. The Sikhs' address lasted at least twenty minutes and HE read out a reply to each one.

We are off this morning for more sightseeing, though there is very little of any real interest in Lahore. Her Ex. was to have motored to the Durbar with Sir M. O'Dwyer who was going to show her to her seat. I thought she would be very huffy at not driving in the procession with HE so I mentioned it to her, after dinner last night, and found she objected to HE driving in a carriage procession without her so I had to tell O'Dwyer, and alter the arrangement. She fairly *bridled* at the idea!!*

Very much love,

Ralph

*Sir Michael O'Dwyer (1864–1940) was Lt-Governor of the Punjab 1913–19. He supported General Dyer after the latter had ordered his troops to fire on what Dyer claimed was an unruly mob at Amritsar in 1919. (see p 159)

April 17th, 1917                                    Viceroy's Camp, India
                                                           Dehra Dun

My own Darling,

We had a very busy day yesterday; the Durbar was a great success. Their Ex.s, Baring and myself drove in the state carriage, the outriders, etc., being in white, instead of the usual red coat. At first HE did not care for the white but after a bit he got used to it and liked it very much indeed. We have never had white before till Lahore. Had it been very hot the red uniforms would have been ruined.

The Durbar lasted for about two hours and about 1,500 Indians came up and were presented to HE, each one offering a gold coin which HE just touched and remitted. He then presented many decorations and badges, and after that made a speech which lasted about twenty minutes. This speech was then read out again in Urdu and the proceedings came to an end. Patiala was the most important chap present and sat on the right of the Viceroy. He was dressed in the most wonderful jewels and was the first to be presented to the Viceroy; then came about six other chaps including Faridkot whom I saw many times.

Yesterday afternoon we spent over two hours at Amritsar and it really is a fascinating place, with very narrow streets and high houses on each side. These narrow streets were very gaily decorated and as we came along we looked right down an avenue of flags crowded with schoolchildren each side, waving flags and yelling at the top of their voices. I never saw so many bands before, but such awful bands, each one playing their own version of the National Anthem. There really were bands every fifty yards!

The Golden Temple was quite lovely, built on a bond in the centre of a large lake. We had to take off our shoes and put on gorgeous slippers. Denny and Baring were in white uniform and could not take off their boots so were not able to come, and could only look on from a kind of platform overlooking the lake.

There were five Sikhs waiting to be baptised in front of the Viceroy. It was not a particularly thrilling ceremony but part of it consisted in the five men feeding each other, absolutely putting the food into the mouths of the others. This is to signify that all castes were done away with and that no matter what rank they were they could eat and feed with other Sikhs. They then bathed in the lake to signify that they were washed clean. In the Golden Temple itself there was a string band of peculiar instruments, and a very High Priest who, with much formality, opened the sacred book and read a few lines out of it for our benefit.

HE had to give Rs. 1,000 to this temple. Patiala has to give no less than Rs. 20,000 when he goes there; the consequence is that he has never been!! He is of course the Head of all the Sikhs, but explained to Sir Michael O'Dwyer that in these hard times he really could not afford the luxury of a visit to the Golden Temple.

Her Ex. went off to the Zenana hospital where she laid a foundation stone, and I went to the Khalsa College which has 700 boys and 400 other students. HE made a short speech, and rather rubbed it into them about volunteering for the service.

They want to get up a double company of 250 students, and the Khalsa College rather prided themselves on the fact that they had supplied twenty-six. HE told them frankly that he did not think that much to buck about, and that there were more than 250 students in front of him, most of whom ought to start the example of enlisting in this Punjab double company, and that he hoped to hear in a day or two that they had done so.

The students seemed rather to like this straight talking as they gave him a jolly good reception at the end of it, though this may have been partly due to the fact that he announced a donation of Rs. 20,000 from Faridkot for the building of a new part of the college.

Your own

Ralph

April 19th, 1917                                        Viceroy's Camp, India

My own Darling,

Yesterday afternoon I got a confidential letter from de Gale asking to be allowed to give up the Body-Guard Command in order to go on active service!! He suggested taking some of the men with him on Service. I wrote back straight away to say that HE desired me to say that he would not stand in his way for a moment, and that he was at liberty to go, and that I was to apply for the services of a light duty officer to relieve him. This drew an immediate reply from de Gale saying that he meant to convey to me that he was only anxious to go on service if he could do so with the Body-Guard!! and asked to be allowed to speak to HE about it. I wrote back that he had better find an opportunity to speak to HE today. I much hope, however, that this may be a solution to the difficulty, and that he will resign with a request to be sent on active service, though he may be sent to his regiment for a bit first.

Your own husband

Ralph

April 21st, 1917                           Viceroy's Camp, India
                                                          Mohand

My own Darling,

This morning the parade was a great success on the whole. The first contretemps was that when the trooper gave the Royal Salute when HE got to the Flagstaff two mounted Nepalese officers in the centre of the line fell off with drawn swords!! First one came off and then the other; they hung on to their reins all right with one hand while, with the other, they pursued their gees with their drawn swords. It looked so fearfully comic that it was all HE could do to stop laughing. We then went down the line in procession like in Calcutta, and by the time we had reached the centre the two officers had resumed their correct positions on the backs of their chargers.

The troops then marched past HE and finally advanced in various order. After the whole show was over, old Baber Shumsheer Jung made a sort of standing speech to HE and then asked permission to call for three cheers for him but HE said 'you may call for three cheers for the King Emperor but not for me,' so Baber Shumsheer Jung rode out in front for a few paces but not near enough for anybody to hear what he was saying, and from a fat white pony stammered out three cheers for the K---ing Hip Hip H-----ooray!! all by himself because nobody knew he was going to do this and so were not prepared for it. However at the third h---ooray a few of them tumbled to what he was trying to do, so faintly joined in. It was one of the most comic things I have ever seen and I suffered agonies trying not to laugh out loud. HE and all of us laughed until we were quite silly when we got home.

However, old Baber was immensely pleased with the whole show and I have this afternoon written him an official letter conveying the Viceroy's very deep satisfaction at everything he saw this morning and saying how much he enjoyed inspecting the Nepalese troops, etc.

Your own

Ralph

# CHAPTER FIVE

In May the Viceroy hears of the death of his son Fred in action. Problems on the N.W. Frontier. Ralph takes a holiday with the Maharajah of Datia. For the first time Indian Officers in the Army are to be treated in the same way as English Officers. Arrangements start being made for Mr Edwin Montagu's visit to India.

In October the Viceroy pays an official visit to Quetta, then they go on to Karachi with more official functions.

Ralph and Nita are to have another baby.

*Ralph to his mother*

May 2nd, 1917                                    Viceregal Lodge, Simla

My dearest Mother,

We got the news of Fred Thesiger's death this morning. I had to
tell HE myself. The C-in-C sent for me about 10 a.m. and said he
wanted to see me at once. I took a rickshaw and went to Army HQ
and the Chief himself handed me the telegram from General Maude
and said he thought I had better be the one to tell the Viceroy. I
came back at once and went in to see HE. It was a dreadful blow to
him. Her Ex. was working downstairs with the Red Cross working
party, so I went to her myself and asked her to come up and see the
Viceroy; I am glad to say she did not ask me anything on the way
up, so I left it to HE to tell her. I then went back again and found
Joan who was working there and I told her on the way up and said
I thought she would like to go in to her mother.*

I think Joan will feel it more than any other member of the family
really, because she and Fred were such great friends. I am afraid
the shock has been all the greater because I do not think any of
them ever worried themselves about Fred, and it never seemed to
occur to them that anything could happen to him.

I do not think the Fête can be postponed on May 19th but
probably the family will all go out to Mashobra for that weekend
and stay there.

Fred was buried at Baghdad yesterday; we have been over-
whelmed with telegrams of condolence. I suppose they will pour in
for the next few days.

                    Your very affectionate

                         Ralph

I think you would like to see this charming letter their Ex.s sent
me. Joan asked if she might come and stay this weekend with us, so
I wrote to find out from Her Ex. if she would mind, and said how
much we would like to have her if we might.

*Frederic Ivor, the Chelmsford's eldest son, died from wounds received in action
in Mesopotania.

Lt-General Sir Stanley Maude (1864–1917) had been Commander-in-Chief in
Mesopotania since August, 1916.

*Lady Chelmsford to Ralph*

(Between 2nd and 4th May, 1917)          Viceregal Lodge, Simla

My dear Ralph,

I am so glad you should have Joan, and if you and Nita can help her through a very difficult and sad time you will be helping us more than I can tell you.

She is so brave and good, and I know it is a great effort to her. She and Fred have always meant so much to each other. I know this house is empty and dreary, and I do feel terribly sad on the girls' account.

It is hard to have to face sorrow so young, and yet the young recover, and there is nothing I wish for more than to see them happily married one of these days – for us, the twenty years can never come again – and just now in one's thoughts one goes over all the episodes in Fred's life and longs to have it all back again. Time will help us – meanwhile the love and sympathy of old friends like yourself is of the greatest value.

Yours affectionately

Frances Chelmsford

*Ralph to his mother*

June 2nd, 1917          Viceregal Lodge, Simla

My dearest Mother,

Last Sunday, Nita and I rode out to a place below Mashobra called Sipi where a great fair is held every year. We had lunch with a Col. and Mrs Burlton. He is Commissioner of Simla. The chief object of this Fair is the buying and selling of wives; although I went with my pockets well lined I did not invest in any more wives! All these women were standing on the ground on the side of the hill in a roped enclosure; I carefully inspected them but could find none to my taste!! The smell for one thing was quite overpowering. Besides this there were sideshows of snake charmers, also of course games and a man dancing, another man shooting arrows between his legs or trying to do so! There were thousands of

Indians there and altogether I thought a show worth seeing once but not twice.

Your affectionate

Ralph

*Ralph to Nita*

June 22nd, 1917                                        Viceregal Lodge, Simla

My own Darling,

HE wanted to know how long I was going to be away for [on holiday]; when I told him till July 2nd he seemed to wonder if it was not rather long for me to be away, so I told him I was at the end of a telephone line and if he sent me a wire to come back I might or might not do so!!! He laughed and said he would try and not risk it.

The Bombay train is being stopped for us at Datia so I shall not have to change at all from Kalka to Datia. Walter will get into my train at Delhi.

I got a wire from the Maharajah of Datia again yesterday evening to say that he was looking forward with much pleasure to my arrival there on the afternoon of the 23rd. So I have sent him a wire this morning to assure him that we are really coming . . .

June 24th, 1917                                        Datia

My own Darling,

We arrived yesterday and were met at the station with great éclat by the Maharajah and his staff on the platform. The train was full of officers going back to Mespot. After we had all said how-do-you-do, an ADC with a bunch of telegrams about a foot high came up and handed them to me. This much surprised Walter until I told him that they were not from the Secretary of State but were all dull and uninteresting Reuters!

Last night the Maharajah and his ADC dined with us and we had a terrible band to play to us the whole evening. It played 'The Roast Beef of Old England' as I led the way into dinner and when I got up to say goodnight to the Maharajah when standing in the garden after dinner, they played the National Anthem.

Tonight we are dining in the Palace with him. It is all very amusing because it is all so very different to Gwalior and in many ways so prehistoric. But HH does all he can to make us comfortable and amuse us, and we are having a very good time.

Very much love, Your own husband

Ralph

*Ralph to his mother*

August 6th, 1917                                    Viceregal Lodge, Simla

My dearest Mother,

I have been very busy with the preparations about our tours this winter. We are going to Quetta, Karachi, Bikanir, Jodhpur, Calcutta, Bombay and Central India with intervals in Delhi but we leave there on Oct. 20th and finally reach Delhi on Jan. 21st. A good many of these visits are official, with public arrivals, which mean a good deal of fixing up, the carriage processions, escorts, salutes, etc. etc.

How frightfully incongruous this does sound when one thinks of all the soldiers in those awful trenches, but still I suppose one must carry on out here, but how much more one would enjoy it all if it was not for the memory of the War always with one.

I am very well. Very much love, Your son

Ralph

*Nita to her father*

August 16th, 1917                                    Viceregal Lodge, Simla

Dearest Father,

Great reforms for home government, etc., are on the tapis. Montagu, our new Secretary of State, is, or was, an ultra radical and the Viceroy and his council are rather in a state of nerves in case he pushes the new reforms too quickly after the splendid work of India in this War; they have got to come but must be set about gradually. On Monday the announcement is to be made that nine Indian Officers are to be given Commissions similar to English officers; they will be able to take the same precedence and rise in just the

same way. This has been debated for forty years and now it has
come, and there is sure to be an enormous amount of opposition
especially from the old Anglo-Indian soldier. I imagine the *Times*
will be swamped by letters from dear old boys living on their
pensions in Battersea and from other Anglo-Indian colonies, tho' I
do not expect it will raise quite such a storm as in pre-war days.
Even the most Conservative organs at home have been much
broader-minded lately and one can't get away from the splendid
loyalty shown by all factions in India these last three years. Even the
Amir has behaved like a trump; he is really at the back of the
complete collapse and surrender of the Mahsuds in our frontier
show the other day. They thought he would be sure to back them up
instead of which he upheld us all thro'.*

My dear love to you all, Your affectionate daughter

Nita

*Edwin Montagu (1879–1924), son of the 1st Lord Swaythling, had been
appointed Secretary of State for India on 17th July. He held the post until March,
1922, when he was obliged to resign for publishing a dispatch from the Indian
Government without Cabinet authority. He was shortly to embark on a tour of India
which resulted in his *Report on Indian Constitutional Reforms*. He "handled his
problems with elasticity and resilience, and by pertinacity, drive and determin-
ation rallied the bulk of opinion to his scheme which passed into law as the
Government of India Act, 1919" (DNB).

This, in consultation with the Viceroy, laid down the Government's policy of
gradual development in India of responsible Government by the Indians
themselves.

*Ralph to his mother*

September 19th, 1917        Viceregal Lodge, Simla

My dearest Mother,

Our winter programme is now rearranged and we leave Delhi on
Nov. 29th for Calcutta, with Mr Montagu and all his party. After ten
days there we go on to Madras and thence to Bombay, returning to
Delhi on Jan. 4th, Gwen's birthday. I am glad to be going to Madras
as I have not been to the south of India before. Her Ex. is only
coming as far as Calcutta with us; the whole trip is a private and
business one, so we shall not be having any public processions, etc.

Most of the time will be taken up with receiving depositions, etc., and giving interviews to various people.

We shall, of course, stay with the Pentlands in Madras; I rather think you know them. I saw Lady Monro this morning who came to listen to the Legislative Council. You may have seen about the speech made the other day in this Council by Sir Michael O'Dwyer, which was considered to be directly opposed in policy to the one made by the Viceroy at the opening meeting of the Council. He did not intend it as such, but still was made by HE to make an apology for it by means of a personal explanation this morning, which caused a good deal of excitement in India; however it all passed off very well, HE getting up and accepting it on behalf of the Council and saying that he hoped Hon. Members would be willing to forego their right of making any remarks about the speech, which of course they had a perfect right to do. It was the Indian members who are chiefly upset and offended by this speech which, in comparing the efforts of the Punjab in the War, passed grave reflections on what had been done in other parts of India, and also gave them to understand that they were by no means ready for any form of responsible Government, etc.*

O'Dwyer is a magnificent man, but rather of the fighting Irishman type. The Viceroy always comes to my office at 9.15 every morning and after showing him my papers which I have to deal with, he usually talks about all kind of things connected with India. By 9.30 a.m. he is back in his room ready to see the surgeon or private secretary, ADC in waiting, etc., but we always have a ten-minute talk about things first, every morning. I am always in my office before 9 o'clock in order to have time to know about any subject I want to discuss with him, such as our tour programmes, military papers that come in, etc. etc. I notice I have mentioned him seeing the surgeon, I do not mean professionally, but very often there are questions relating to hospitals, etc., in India, which his surgeon deals with.

The ADC in waiting goes to him every morning to find out what HE wishes to do for that day and to warn him about any engagements he has got, which he then sends to me in writing for my information. The ADC in waiting on Her Ex. does the same at 10 a.m. and finds out if she wants the carriage at any time or what their plans are for the day. I am always in my office until 1 o'clock when I usually go away for an hour back to lunch here. I find I hardly ever have to be in office after 4.30 p.m. and then I nearly always play tennis with HE in our covered court, which is an excellent game.

Of course on tour one is on the go all day, and always in the evening up to 11 p.m. or later, but certainly the touring is the most interesting part of my job and the most amusing, provided things go all right. I have been asked by the Home Dept. to be responsible for the travelling arrangements for Mr Montagu the whole time he is in India, so have to arrange for his special train, etc., up from Bombay.

I am pitching a huge camp at Viceregal Lodge, Delhi, for him and his party and am making them very comfortable with brick fireplace, new furniture, etc. I do not think he will realize he is in a tent at all when he gets inside. I cannot help wishing it was Mr Chamberlain who was coming out but I expect Mr Montagu will make himself agreeable all right. There are four others coming out with him besides his own private secretary. From the day he gets to Delhi which might be about Nov. 7th we shall be with him every single day he is in India. He is not going to be allowed to go on tour by himself at all. Our only big function on tour is the Jan. 1st parade in Bombay when the Viceroy is to give a good many War Service Decorations.

Your affectionate son

Ralph

*John Sinclair, 1st Lord Pentland (1860–1925) was Governor of Madras 1912 – 19.

Lady Munro was the daughter of the 1st Lord O'Hagan. Her husband, General Sir Charles (1860–1929), was Commander-in-Chief, India 1916–20.

*Ralph to Nita*

September 21st, 1917                    Viceregal Lodge, Simla

My own Darling,

Of course, O'Dwyer's type of speech will always be the popular type among Englishmen who have not got to bear the responsibility of Government on their shoulders and who are naturally opposed to

giving any concessions to Indians, but granting that these concessions have got to come, and that this Viceroy has got to bring
them in, I do not think any man worth his salt could have allowed
that speech to pass without remark, and O'Dwyer was the first
man to realize and acknowledge that himself. O'Dwyer is under the
Viceroy, and after the Viceroy's own speech and also after the
definite announcement of the object of Montagu's visit, it looked
something very like insubordination on O'Dwyer's part to make a
speech like that, not to mention disloyalty to the Viceroy himself, or
perhaps a disloyal attempt to curry favour with the British public
out here at the Viceroy's expense.

Knowing perfectly well what the policy of the Government of
India now is, and has to be, O'Dwyer must either loyally help to
carry it out or resign. There is no question about that at all to my
mind.

I should much like to be able to have a talk to Deane about it, but
this is how it strikes me, though I know very well that this will not
appeal to the English officer in the Indian Army, just as he will be
equally seriously opposed to the granting of these commissions. But
both things have got to come, and I am quite sure that the Viceroy
is certain to incur the hostility and dislike of very many people in
consequence, and to be called weak.

He is just as much bound to try and carry out the policy of the
Secretary of State and the Government at Home in these matters, as
those who are subordinate to him are bound to support him in doing
so or resign. If you see Deane again and he talks about it, you can
read out to him what I have written, and I am perfectly sure that he
will agree with this view of the case, however seriously he may
disagree with the policy itself.

No time for more now,
Very much love, Your own

Ralph

October 27th, 1917                                    Viceroy's Camp, Quetta

My own Darling,

We had a splendid day yesterday shooting chikhor. After sleeping
in the train for the night, we motored for about 15 miles to the

shooting ground and then walked for about five miles altogether. We came back to a most sumptuous camp, with an excellent lunch, and then some of us including HE motored the whole way back to Quetta, about forty-five miles. I never saw such a deserted and dreary country in my life, nothing but steep, bare hills without a single tree or a single house of any kind, nothing but rock and bare sandy red-coloured ground. However, it was very interesting coming back by motor, and quicker than the train.

We are now just off to the Prize-giving show at the Cadet College. We have the Fête in aid of our 'Day' this afternoon and leave Quetta this evening.

I received another cheque from Alwar for 10,000 Rs for 'Our Day'. Her Ex. simply could not remember if she had written to thank him for this huge donation or not. I had to wire off to Gould to try and find out if he knew whether she had written or not. We have just come back from the Fête at which Their Ex.s spent over 500 Rs.

I have really been most awfully busy this time, and have not had time for anything. This morning, for instance, it was reported to me that some of our servants, while we were away, yesterday went to the Khan of Khalat and another chief, demanding backsheesh and got 250 Rs from one and 35 Rs from the other. I held an investigation immediately after lunch, and when I had found out all about it, held a sort of Court, with Maffey, in a tent. I sacked four of them straight away, and extracted nearly 200 Rs from their purses there and then. I got hold of the official Receipt for the money signed by one of the men, but it all took some time and gave me a lot of bother; I do not think any of our servants will try that game on again. Two of the men were out of Maffey's own office and are under arrest for tonight, and are being sent off on the train tomorrow.

I am awfully sorry that Mrs Young had such a bad time. I would not let you have a baby under Mickey for anything in the world, but I do really trust Cuffs [Col. Austen Smith]. I know he will do everything he possibly can for you. I think Biddy and Joan might do something about Marthe when we get back again to Delhi, but I am not going to mix myself up in it at all.

Your own

Ralph

November 1st, 1917                              Viceroy's Camp, Karachi

My own Darling,

We got a wire from Montagu today to say that he expected to reach Bombay on the morning of the 9th, so I shall be starting off from Delhi on the 6th which is the very day you arrive; I shall probably be able to meet you at the station in the motor, return to the bungalow with you, have breakfast and then go off to catch my train. [Nita had been away on a three weeks' holiday in a rickshaw near Tibet.]

We had a most successful dinner at the Club last night, and HE was quite at the top of his form; he spoke very frankly to the members saying that he felt he could do so because he was sure that nothing which he said to them would appear in the Press or be repeated outside the Club. He stuck up very strongly for Sir W. Meyer and talked a good deal about finance, saying that in India we had no policy of our own as regards finance, as our policy now was an Imperial policy, and that we in India were only anxious to co-operate with the authorities at home in order to bring this War to a conclusion.[1]

Then he talked quite freely about Mrs Besant. He put forward one point of view which was new to me and I think new to everybody there, namely that it may be wise for us to start these schemes of reform now, when we know that we have at home a Government with moderate views, as if we waited and put off bringing in these schemes of reform till a later date it might be quite possible that by that time we had a government at home whose views would be much more violent, and who might urge us on to still greater reforms, rather than check a moderate new scheme which may be put before them.[2]

HE also stuck up for Montagu and told the members quite frankly that all the hostility to his visit was purely personal on the part of the English people in India, and that not a single word of protest would have been heard if it had been Chamberlain who was coming out. HE said that the proverb of the dog having a bad name might be applied in this case, but that if they wanted to criticize or blame anybody let them do it to the man on the spot which was himself, and not behind the back of the man who was not there to defend himself. He got a great reception on leaving the Club, all the members cheered him loudly. The general feeling after dinner was that HE's speech had cleared the air and by appealing to them all to do what they could to help, and not to hinder himself and Mr Montagu in solving the great problems in front of them, I think he won everybody over to his side without a doubt.

You have not yet told me what Nurse thinks of the possibility of a new baby and whether she likes the idea more than I do!!

Your own

Ralph

[1]Sir William Stevenson Meyer (1860–1922) was Finance Minister, Government of India 1913–18. He became the first High Commissioner of India in 1922.
[2]Annie Besant (1847–1933) was a pupil of Mme Blavatsky and joined the Theosophical Society of which she became President in 1907. In 1916 she initiated the Home Rule for India League. She claimed that her adopted son, Krishnamurti, was the Messiah. A personal and entertaining account of Mrs Besant's "mission" is to be found in Viscount Churchill's autobiography, *All My Sins Remembered* (Heinemann, 1964)

# CHAPTER SIX

In November the Viceroy returns to Delhi, Ralph goes to Bombay to meet Montagu and his entourage. He takes them to Delhi and then on to Calcutta where Montagu, between working on his report on India with the Viceroy, manages to get some sport. In the middle of December they all go on to Madras with a continuing mixture of official engagements, receptions and sport.

Just before Christmas the Viceroy visits Shahabad, staying with the Governor there, Lord Willingdon, with more official functions before returning to Delhi in early January 1918 while his party visits the Maharajah of Patiala, and Nita and family are invited to stay with the Maharajah of Gwalior. A further Council of Indian Chiefs in Delhi in February with more official engagements, relieved by some sport when it can be fitted in.

*Ralph to his mother*

November 16th, 1917                    Viceregal Lodge, Delhi

My darling Mother,

   I am sorry to say Nita is in bed with a go of fever which is very annoying; personally I do not think it is malaria but the result of a chill she got at the Chief's banquet, but the blood is to be tested today. She hopes very much to be able to go to Bikanir next week, but we will have to see how she is.

   I went to Bombay and met the Secretary of State and his party there, and brought them back to Delhi by special train. I stayed at the Taj Mahal Hotel and had one spare day there. Lord Willingdon came to meet them and we all lunched and dined that day at the Bombay Yacht Club. Lord Donoughmore knows Joan and Harry (Verney) very well. He is great fun, very fit and rather a wag. Mr Roberts, MP, knew the other Harry quite well, and of course Mr Montagu also. The latter told me how he had asked that Harry should be invited to tea to meet him at HQ in France. Kirsch, the private secretary, has got a bald head but long black hairs parted right down over his ears, and then brushed across to hide the baldness, a style of coiffure I particularly dislike!! Parsons, the assistant private secretary, is quite nice but looks like an actor; he married Viola Tree, the daughter of the actor, and has very long hair brushed back over his head. I happened to see him the other day as he came out of his bath, and none of his face was visible at all. I have had long talks with all of them, and it is interesting to hear their account of how things are at home. It makes us realize how lucky we are to be out in India where we have no difficulty about petrol, sugar, coal, etc. I like Mr Montagu very much personally, and he is very nice about trying to give as little trouble as possible. They were all very amusing about their tents; I rather rubbed it in on the way up from Bombay that I hoped they would not be very uncomfortable living in tents. When we took them after breakfast to their respective tents they could only stand and stare. We had made them very comfortable with beautiful carpets; a nice bright fire was burning in each tent in a proper brick fireplace, there were sofas, proper windows and double doors, palms, very good writing-tables, etc. I think they expected something in the nature of a bell tent or even a little bivouac! These gorgeous Viceregal tents come as a real eye-opener to them, with their telephones and electric light, and cameras were at once unpacked in order that they might be photographed.[1]

We have started with Deputations yesterday; they started at 10.30 a.m. and finished up at 7 p.m. The Viceroy is here for the depositions but not for the interviews. It is really an awful waste of time for him because all the addresses are written out and he could quite well read them in his room, but it is thought better that he should receive all these depositions with the Secretary of State.

We start off for Calcutta on the 29th and do not get back here till Jan 4th.

It is a great joy having my motor again. It is running very well and I have got the same Indian chauffeur as last year.

The Russian news gets worse every day, it is impossible to keep pace with their changes of government in Petrograd. The Chiefs' conference went off very well; I was away for most of it. A good many were asked to stay on in Delhi till the following Tuesday in order to meet Mr Montagu, and we had an evening party here on the Monday night to which they all came in their best bibs and tuckers, not to mention jewels.

Very much love,
Your very affectionate

Ralph

[1]Richard Walter John Hely-Hutchinson, 6th Earl of Donoughmore (1875–1948) was Chairman of Committees and Deputy Speaker of the House of Lords 1911–31.

Charles Henry Roberts (1865–1959) had been Under-secretary of State for India 1914–15. He was Liberal MP for Lincoln 1906–18. In 1917 he was invited, with the Earl of Donoughmore, to accompany Mr Edwin Montagu on his official visit to India.

Alan Parsons (1887–1933) had married Viola, daughter of Sir Herbert Beerbohm Tree in 1912. He was Private Secretary to Edwin Montagu, having been exempted from military service on account of his asthma.

November 29th, 1917                          Viceregal Lodge, Delhi

My dearest Mother,

I am off to Calcutta tomorrow, but just send you a line to catch the mail tomorrow.

In January, after our return from tour, there is going to be a big Round Table conference for the Secretary of State. I have got to put up no less than eight Governors, etc.; if they only bring one member of their staff each that means sixteen guests besides the Secretary of State and his party, and also the Thesiger family from Abyssinia who are coming to stay with four sons from three to eight years of age, so the house party for that week will be pretty big!!

Splendid news has come in this morning from East Africa; it really looks as though that campaign might come to an end before so very long which will release a good many of our troops who, after a stay in India of six months or so, ought to be fit for service again somewhere else.

Your very affectionate

Ralph


December 6th, 1917                    Viceroy's Camp, Calcutta, India

My own Darling,

I was horrified this morning when Her Ex. made another attempt to come with us to Madras! I was not at all cordial about the suggestion and she had to own that she had not had the courage to mention it to HE!! It would be too bad of her to alter her whole plans at the last moment like this, and of course she would have to come to Bombay too, but I sincerely hope she will not broach the subject to HE at all, after the way I pointed out to her the trouble it will cause, but you never know, she is quite capable of doing so, and of course she hates being left out of anything.

I have got to take her all over Belvedere this morning. I went over it the other day and think it quite possible to arrange it for the Viceroy to live in for a fortnight or so next year, without running into too much money. Hastings House which I inspected yesterday is quite out of the question; it is now used as a school and is not nearly as suitable as Belvedere.

I am having a struggle with the Secretary of State about coming to the races on our Day; he loathes racing which I told him quite frankly was no excuse, then he said he was too busy, on which I said if he arranged interviews on that afternoon he would be preventing other people going to the Races who ought to be there.

On which he said he only wanted to see Lord Curtis. The real
reason why he does not want to go is that he is frightened of being
bombed!! It seems quite incredible, but it is true all the same. And
I want to take him there if only for half an hour in order to show
him how very ridiculous that idea is, but he is an obstinate old
thing and I may not succeed in getting him there, but I shall do so
if I can possibly manage it. Everybody in Calcutta expects him to
be there and I think he would be very foolish indeed if he refused
to go . . .


December 8th, 1917                    Viceroy's Camp, Calcutta, India

My own Darling,

I have been chaffing the life out of that Mr Roberts who went out
last night with L. Curtis and a parson here, to have a look at the
public houses in the low part of Calcutta. I told him this morning at
breakfast that he woke me up at 8.30 a.m. coming back in a noisy
cab from his night out. Nobody more unlikely to have ever had a
night out I cannot conceive; he is frightfully keen about teetotal-
ism, and all the evil of the public houses in England. We asked
him if his experiences last night were going to be embodied in Mr
Montagu's report!

The ADCs here have got up an Address to Montagu which is
going to be read out to him by Balfour on Monday night, after the
dinner party, when all the guests have gone. It is being properly
printed on vellum and is I believe going to be encased in a small
model thunderbox!! It speaks of the hardships which have to be
endured by members of the ADC Association in the matter of
travelling allowances which they are not allowed to draw, also
of the iniquitous system which forces them to attend with the
Governor the meetings of the Legislative Council, but forbids them
to enjoy the privilege of voting at the same, etc. We were careful to
make them show us the rough draft of it beforehand, in case they
put anything objectionable in it!! I think it also contains an expression of satisfaction at the weighty support which the Delegation has
enjoyed in the presence of the rotund Donoughmore!! After this
address has been read, Balfour is to present all the ADCs by name
to the Secretary of State who will shake hands with them and then

he is expected to make a reply, and is to be told that the stereo-typed answer that due consideration would be given, etc., would not be accepted on this occasion!

Your own

Ralph

December 11th, 1917                    Viceroy's Camp, India

My own Darling,

Last night after dinner the ADCs presented their address to Mr Montagu. I have sent you a copy of it today. Balfour read it out and read it most awfully well; then he presented the members of the deputation, but the whole thing was a frost because instead of making a clever and witty reply, to every one's astonishment he just got up, said 'Thank you, Gentlemen', and walked out of the room!! He was given the Address wrapped up in a very nice old Thibetan Banner which Balfour provided, and I really think he might have played up and made a little speech in reply. Something upset him either before or after dinner, as I do not think there was anything in the Address to which he could really take exception. The whole thing was a joke but I am afraid it fell awfully flat in the end . . .

December 18th, 1917                    Viceroy's Camp, Madras, India

My own Darling,

I got a wire at dinner last night from Parsons to say that Her Ex. had cancelled the Dehra Dun visit. I sent it to the Viceroy last night and he was jolly sick about it this morning, and went straight to his table to write to Her Ex. about it. When in Calcutta she tried, as I told you, to come down here and also to Bombay but I was not 'taking any'! When she got back to Delhi she wired to the Willingdons on her own, suggesting going there for Xmas, but got a snub for her pains as they wired back that they regretted that they could not alter the arrangements at the moment, and would not have room to put her up. I suppose she got the huff and decided if she could not go to Bombay she would not go anywhere, 'Nobody loves me' sort of attitude; she really is the limit. I know that the whole reason why the Willingdons will not have her was that Her Ex. never answered that letter from Lady W. which she got in Simla, inviting her and Joan to Bombay for Xmas, and then when Her Ex. proposed herself at the last moment, Lady W. would naturally say, 'No, I am blowed if I would have her now'. I only hope HE wrote to her pretty straight. He was very annoyed about it this morning, saying that it was really too bad of Her Ex. to upset the plans like this . . .

December 20th, 1917            Viceroy's Camp, Madras, India

My own Darling,

We had such a dull garden party yesterday. But a man called Pumffrey in the uniform of a Captain in the RB came up to me and introduced himself and his wife. He was a corporal and then a sergeant in the 2nd Batt. and went out to S.A. on the old *Umbria* with me in March 1900. He was in A Company and was with me the whole time in Egypt, and also at Shahjehanpur and Chanbattia. He left the Battalion to go on the staff in Calcutta and during the war has been given a commission and is now Adjutant of some railway volunteers in Madras. I remember his name perfectly but never knew him well myself as he was not in my Company. We had such a long buck together about the regiment and all the old 2nd Batn officers and NCOs. His wife was equally keen about the regiment, and both came out to India with the 2nd Batn. in 1905 and he has been here ever since with one trip home . . .

December 22nd, 1917            Viceroy's Camp, Madras

My own Darling,

I have been this morning with Hale, one of the ADCs here, to look over a cigar factory, and very interesting it was. I have come back with two large boxes of cigars, each box containing four different sorts, twenty-five of each sort. We saw the whole process of cigar making right from the beginning. It was curious to see the way the Indian uses his toes as easily as I use my fingers, holding one end of a long cigar leaf in his toes and then rolling the cigar up in the leaf with his fingers. Another man spends his life in packing them up in bundles of twenty-five, tied together with a yellow ribbon; he picks up twenty-five cigars in his hands without ever counting them and never makes a mistake. Most of the work was done by hand, in the most dirty-looking hovels in rather a back street; nearly 400 men being employed and working at the same thing from 6 a.m. to 1 p.m. and from 2 p.m. to 10 p.m., fifteen hours' work a day, but they are paid piece work rates and prefer to work like that and then knock off altogether for sometimes a week at a time; for instance, they close tomorrow till the 2nd January. The man who runs the place now is a Mr Hooper whose family came from near Amersham. This firm sent home ten cigar makers to work at the Earl's Court Exhibition, the year that the Great Wall was put up. I saw the man who went home as the chief worker, and he had sat for many weeks in one of those stalls at the exhibition, making cigars; I daresay I saw him there myself.

We had a very successful opening of the Industrial Exhibition yesterday afternoon. Mr Innes who was chairman of the Exhibition Campaign asked me if I did not come from Claydon; he has stayed there many times and remembered me perfectly there in 1904; he is a friend of Aunt Margy's and used to come over from Oxford. I remembered his name perfectly and have a sort of vague recollection of him.*

I have been distributing presents all the morning. I had rather a job to get the Viceroy to give his photo to Lord P. [Pentland] because the former did not think that it was wanted. He thinks that Lord P. is rather sore about the Besant incident and that although he would not allow himself to show it, he is not really very cordial to HE. I do not agree with him and got the photo given all right.

Lord P. heard the Viceroy liked a particular kind of cigar and sent the whole way to Trichinopoly and got 500 as a present for him. He is a most awfully kind person. So we return from Madras loaded up with cigars.

Your own

Ralph

*Aunt Margy was 'Claydon' Harry Verney's mother. Claydon was also the name of the family home near Aylesbury.

December 24th, 1917                    Viceroy's Camp, Bombay, India

My own Darling,

We got here after a good journey at 8.30 and the depositions started at 10 a.m. so not much time was wasted.

At a place called Shahabad, yesterday we were given a tremendous luncheon by the Nizam of Hyderabad who sent his chief minister there to act as host. Two triumphal arches had been built, shamianas erected, etc. etc., two motor cars sent to take HE and the Sec. of State from the station to the Shamiana, the distance being about 100 yards! Mr Fraser and his personal accountant, a nice man called Cater, got on the train about twenty miles before. The former's two daughters and the latter's granddaughter are at Hyderabad.

Everything here is much the same; there seem to be any number of ADCs running about all over the place, one has just popped in to find out if I want anything!! I felt inclined to ask for a glass of champagne or an iced cocktail!!

Lady Willingdon was most gracious to me this morning and said, 'Oh, how delightful it is to have you again'!!!!! She is a *humbug*. I really am rather glad that Her Ex. is not here because we are frightfully busy without having to look after her; there are so many calls to be paid, the Jan.1st parade to be arranged, depositions and interviews all day and every day. Also she would have been the only lady in the party on the train, which I think would have been rather a mistake; however my gain is, I am afraid, at your expense!

I have got Xmas presents from HE for all the staff here. I mean the Willingdon staff, instead of giving them presents when we leave; it is a much nicer plan. Very nice silver cigarette boxes, etc., with Xmas 1917 engraved in them and their initials.

Your own

Ralph

Xmas Day, 1917                              Viceregal Camp, Bombay

My own Darling,

I thought of you this morning as soon as I woke up, and expect you went into the Nursery to help the children with their parcels?!! Biffy and Bunting were delighted with their parcels – which they had with their early tea. I sat next to Lady W. at breakfast this morning, and without the others hearing, got straight on to the subject of her letter to Her Ex. which was never answered. She said she was sorry she could not upset her arrangements at the last moment at Her Ex.'s request as she fully realized that Her Ex. would sooner be here than left by herself in Delhi, but that having asked her and Joan to come here and having heard definitely through me that they would not be coming, she had arranged otherwise.

I really found it very difficult to give any explanation about her letter not having been answered, so changed the subject as soon as I could, but I could perfectly clearly see that Lady W. was anything but pleased with Her Ex. about it. I only hope she does not mention the matter to HE who would be highly sick with Her Ex.

This morning HE came to me and said to me he had been told by the Jemadar he could not have his breakfast in his room!! I very soon put that right, but the servants would not serve breakfast in his room because Lady W. had not ordered it.

I get quite a lot of quiet fun out of staying here, I can tell you. Last night after dinner Lady W. told Greenway that the Viceroy never said goodnight to the guests but just left quietly by himself to go to bed; Greenway asked Biffy if this was so who, of course, said HE always said goodnight to the guests. In order to prove she was right Lady W. came over to him, stood for a few minutes with him and then just marched him off to bed through the billiard room, without saying goodnight to anybody. I tackled her about it this morning and she said she thought HE looked tired, and decided to send him straight to bed without bothering to say goodnight!! I do not think there is a single member of this staff who dare say a word to her!!*

Very much love,
Your own

Ralph

*Charles Greenway (1888–1963) succeeded his father as 2nd Baron Greenway in 1934. He was Military Secretary to the Governor of Bombay 1916–17; Commandant Bombay Bodyguard 1917–18.

December 27th, 1917            Viceroy's Camp, India
Bombay

My own Darling,

I got your letter this morning about what Mrs Maffey had said to you. I really felt I could not allow that to pass. I went after a bath straight to Maffey, and I told him perfectly straight that if we were going to pull together as a staff I could not possibly allow Mrs Maffey to take up that attitude. I read out to him certain parts of your letter; he was absolutely grovelling with apology though he absolutely denied having written anything to his wife such as she claimed. I must say he was awfully nice and took it very well, as I spoke out my mind to him very straight. He of course saw how absurd it was for her to think I had anything to do at all with Her Ex. not coming here. The very first I heard of the telegram she sent was when Maffey told me himself about it. It was quite incorrect to say that she would have caused no trouble if she did come, because Lady W. herself refused to upset her arrangements in order to have her. For instance, all the printing in connection with the list of guests and their rooms had been done already, so Lady W. could not get it altered even if she had pushed to do so. Lady W. told me this herself. I simply do not believe Her Ex. when she says HE expressed a wish that she should come, or in any way gave his consent to her trying to work it herself.

About Lady W.'s letter, I can only say that Lady W. has tackled me about it since I have been here, so it is very clear that she considered it as a definite invitation which was never replied to, also Her Ex. acknowledged to me that she had received it when I asked her about it in Delhi, on my return from Bombay. Considering that I was in Madras when Her Ex. sent that wire from Delhi, I do not quite know how I could have been responsible for getting Lady W. to refuse to have her here, especially as I did not know anything at all about this plan of hers. It is quite true that I threw cold water when she suggested it the last day in Calcutta, and what happened proves that I was quite right in trying to dissuade her from trying to propose herself, because I knew quite well what Lady W.'s reply would be under the circumstances.

She has got nobody to blame but herself and I do not think Mrs Maffey will try that game on again. I have never spoken like that to Maffey before, and I sincerely hope I shall never have to again, but I was determined he should have quite frankly from me what I thought of the attitude taken up by his wife. I claimed as a team we had played pretty well together for two years and I was not going to have our apple cart upset by his wife.

It is part of my job to save Her Ex. from putting her feet into it, as she did by sending that wire from Delhi, and it was only when she got back to Delhi that she was silly enough to try and work it that she should come to Bombay, and she got a snub for her pains. However, if this whole storm in a teacup cleared the air as far as Mrs Maffey is concerned, some good will have come out of it!!! . . .


December 29th, 1917                     Viceroy's Camp, India
                                                          Bombay

My own Darling,

I went to such an awfully interesting place here yesterday evening, namely the Parel Institute where all kinds of experiments are being carried out. The most interesting thing we saw was a poison being extracted from the fangs of cobras and of Russell Vipers; these snakes are in different boxes. The man who was going to do it brought out one of these boxes into the middle of the room and put it on a mat. He opened the lid and let out the snake. He had a bamboo stick in his left hand and quickly pressed the head of the snake down to the floor by putting this bamboo stick across its neck. He took the tail of the snake with his right hand and put it under his bare foot. Thus the snake was held flat out on the ground. Then, with his right hand, he got hold of the snake just behind its head and held it up firmly between his thumb and his fingers with its mouth wide open and hissing with anger. Another man brought an ordinary wine glass covered over with some black calico; the glass was put close to the mouth of the snake who bit at it viciously; his fangs went through the calico and the poison poured out into the wine glass: about ten or twelve drops of a slightly yellow liquid. I never knew a snake had such long sharp teeth; one could see the poison oozing from these fangs; then the snake was fed by putting a funnel down its throat and an egg flip was poured down it!! He lives on this egg flip for a whole week.

Very much love, my own darling,
Your own

Ralph

*Ralph to his mother*

January 6th, 1918                    Viceregal Lodge, Delhi

My dear Mother,

I got back here on Friday morning, and except for weekends shall be settled in Delhi till towards the end of March. It was most bitterly cold the day I got back and we have fires going in our sitting-room all day.

Nita and the children are very much better than when I left, also Nurse. Nita wrote to you last week and told you our exciting news; she is most awfully pleased at the prospect of another baby which ought to make its appearance towards the end of May. Col. Austen Smith, the Viceroy's Surgeon, will look after her; he is very good and very careful and absolutely on the spot as he lives less than ten minutes' walk away from us in Simla, so I have every hope that all will go well. We shall have to try and get hold of a nursery maid as Shaw cannot possibly manage three children.

Your affectionate son

Ralph

*Ralph to his cousin, Harry Lloyd Verney*

January 16th, 1918                    Viceregal Lodge, Delhi

My dear old Harry,

You did let yourself go in your 'private' letter to Nita, dated December 3rd!! You may, of course, be perfectly right about Harrow and its disastrous results on the youthful unfortunates committed to its tender care, and if things are as bad as you make out, I should certainly agree with you that the sacrifice entailed on my sons by sticking to our family Harrow tradition was not good enough, and I should prefer to send them to Eton or Winchester; by-the-by Donoughmore, though an old Etonian, refused to send his sons to Eton and sent them to Winchester!!

However, there is luckily plenty of time yet before I need take the final plunge of severing the family connection with Harrow.

Let me now turn to another part of your letter, with which I am by no means in such complete agreement with you.

I am by no means convinced that there is bound to be another large War, as you appear to be; one of the objects we are fighting for now, according to the Prime Minister (for whom you have always had such a strong feeling of personal affection!) is that never again may we have to undergo the horrors of a European War. I may be quite wrong, but my firm conviction is that if peace came tomorrow, there would not be another big War in our time, in our sons' time, nor yet in our grandsons' time, and for this reason – that those who do the fighting now are going to do the voting in the future, and those who have had any experience of what modern Warfare means, and who are going to vote for a repetition of it, are going to be in a jolly small minority, whether they are English, French or German!

By this I do not mean that there should be complete training for everyone. I am entirely in favour of some kind of universal training for every single young man in the whole Empire, but I certainly do not go as far as you say, as you do, that the only possible professions in the future 'for boys of your class and mine' are the Army and the Navy, and possibly the Diplomatic Service or the ICS.

My dear Harry, you mention Commerce as our ancestors might have mentioned it in the early days of Queen Victoria!

Take our two nicest ADCs; Holland Hibbert was at Eton, but sad to relate went into business, namely Lloyds. Baring was at Eton, but sad to relate, disgraced his old school by going into the family banking business; I honestly do not think either of them can be said not to belong to your class and mine, nor do I think they have in any way suffered by their connection with the commercial circles you so heartily despise!

Don't imitate old Diogenes, but come out of your scry aristocratic tub and have a look at the world as it is today; be as much of a Tory as you like, but don't quote early Victorian sentiments in 1918, for it won't work! If you were to come out to this country now, I could show you several garrison Battalions doing duty in India, whose officers are mostly composed of businessmen; take our own 24th Bat. Rifle Brigade at Agra; hardly a subaltern of under fifty years of age; a Lieut. Pawle, over sixty, with four sons fighting, and now himself in Mesopotamia; at the beginning of the War a flourishing business man on the London Stock Exchange!

I do not agree with you for a moment, that it is necessary for our sons to go into the Army or the Navy in order to prove that they are loyal subjects of the King; it is possible for a businessman to be just as patriotic as any soldier or sailor.

If you agree as I think you must, that commerce is of the first-rate importance to the British Empire, then surely it is a good thing that among the men who are engaged in Commerce should be included a fair percentage of what you and I mean by 'the sons of gentlemen'.

One thing which would certainly weigh with me against sending John to Eton would be the thought that he would be educated and trained there to grow up in the out of date, not to say snobbish, sentiments expressed in your letter to Nita; but I have too many Eton friends to believe that for a moment. I stick to the hope that the various branches of the commercial business of the Empire may still have their quota of old Etonians in the future, as they have had in the past.

I do not mark my letter 'private' because I really do not mind who sees it!!

Write again soon, I hope you will, in spite of this letter!!*

My very best love to your Joan and yourself,
Always yours affectionately

Ralph

---

*At the time of this letter Harry Lloyd was Deputy Master of HM's. Household and his wife Joan was one of Queen Mary's Ladies-in-Waiting.

Ralph did send his sons to Eton; the eldest became a writer and artist, and the younger – why, he went into the Navy and then did twenty-eight years managing a China Clay Company in Cornwall before starting on these letters!

*Ralph to his mother*

January 23rd, 1918                    Viceregal Lodge, Delhi

My dearest Mother,

On February 1st, I am going off with the Secretary of State to Dholpur, for Saturday and Sunday. Donoughmore is coming too.

We have got all the governors and Lt. Governors here now and we are forty-five or more for every meal. We have got actually staying with us Mr Gourlay, the private secretary in Calcutta, a Capt. Greenway, the military Secretary in Bombay, also a Mr Alexander in the Ghurka regiment whom I have taken on for a month as extra ADC and who was for eighteen months a prisoner in Germany.

Very much love,
Your very affectionate

Ralph

*Nita to Ralph's mother*

February 1st, 1918                    The State Guest House, Gwalior

My dear Mother,

Your letters of Dec. 10th and 18th have just arrived; you will be surprised to see the above address.

This has been a most unique visit. The Maharajah of Scindia is a most generous little man and so very human; his love of practical jokes and kindnesses are known all over India. It was he who sent the children such lovely toys. We are now his guests in the guest house close to the palace, the most colossal palace I have ever seen.

Yesterday I took Nurse and the children to call on the Maharanis, there are two, the first a very clever woman to whom he was married for twenty years; there were no children so four years ago he married another girl and now has a boy and a girl, George and Mary. The King and Queen are their godparents though they are most orthodox Hindus!! George is a funny little scrap of eighteen months, Mary a most old-fashioned little piece of three. She goes and meets her father's guests at the station and gives away prizes at functions; she has her own motor and carriage and a guard, and a band of little boys who surround her carriage or motor and play as she commands downstairs. The four children are tremendously taken with each other; in fact my two formed up and embraced George. Most embarrassing, and they looked such bulky giants in com- parison. I always thought Joscelyne a dainty little person before, but she seems massive and clumsy besides Mary.

The Maharanis have their separate apartments. The Senior one was entertaining several people to tea and very much at her ease, the other seemed very shy and sat upon, poor little girl; I have learnt a lot about her today from a Mrs Stephens, their companion and doctor and secretary all rolled into one, but who has been in the palace for twenty years. The old Maharani mother-in-law has complete charge of the children and the senior Maharani wife, who takes precedence, always holds the children at any palace ceremonies and presents them as OUR children to the visitors, while the real mother stands in the background and says nothing, and she is so devoted to them, and longs to be allowed to play with them alone and dress them. Both children have wonderful pearl earrings and strings of pearls just like those you gave me, with the same settings. Mrs Stephens brought them both into the world and told me what difficulties she had to face. They could not be born into anything white and their mother could not wear white, so clean sheets and night gowns were out of the question. The room was packed with women arranged about by their ranks, and at the back stood the astrologer who immediately cast the child's horoscope as it entered the world.

The wife was chosen entirely because her horoscope fitted in with the Maharajah's very favourably; she comes from a poor but noble family but not Royal.

Much love from your daughter

Nita

*From Ralph's sister*

March 3rd, 1918 Botolph House, Claydon

My dearest Nita,

You ask about the rationing. I confess I do find it rather difficult to give the family things they like. It isn't nearly so bad when you

have twelve people to feed (our number) as for quite small house-
holds, because the total of the rations goes a long way in the case
of fats, etc., for cooking. I find Mother much the most difficult
member of the family to feed, though I don't tell her so. We all
manage the substitutes very well – margarine instead of butter, oil
for cakes instead of margarine, potato instead of suet, etc., but
Mother doesn't like the results, though our Mrs Norman manages as
well as she can. I see her putting pudding in her spoon or just not
taking any. Of course I arrange for there always to be something I
know she will eat, but even so I cannot always manage something
she will like.

K. [Ralph's sister] and I don't mind, and I see to it that the
children's food is the same as it always was. The milk ration isn't in ·
force yet in this district, and with plenty of garden vegetables and
still a vast store of bottled fruit from what I did last summer, we are
really very well off.

I think it is most interesting how the War is compelling us to
cultivate, of late, in quite a different way to what was done before.
Round here there is quite a lot of ploughed land now, and therefore
no doubt it is giving a good impetus to all farming and gardening
*except* flowers! Every bit of ground is dug up and looked after, and
of course a great deal is done by women. Ralph would be interested
to hear that Mr Perry has got one of the women on the land in the
outfit of her kind: thick smock over leather gaiters and breeches.
She is such a very nice girl, and I like her immensely. Harriet at
Granborow has one lodging with her in old Jays; I would have
thought she was much too old fashioned to wish to HOUSE anyone
of that sort, but the girls don't even get stared at now.

Then the Board of Agriculture is sending free lecturers all over
the country to tell people how to manage their crops and
particularly allotments. Some of the people they engage are local
people with a good working knowledge of the subject, gardeners or
smallholders. We had a teacher in the Hall here a week ago and of
course I went, being very keen to hear and learn more about the
succession of vegetables, as most of the garden is given up to them
now.

I can't tell you how dreadfully funny it was, and I suffered pains
and aches from suppressed laughter. The chairman was a very old
man from Winslow, a gardener, and he gave a long discourse on the

nature of root crops, when we were longing to hear the speaker. In the middle he said, 'Ladies and gentlemen, I have a most peculiar stomach and it is coming on now.' He rubbed himself in front and then subsided into his chair, whereupon the speaker took his chance, jumped up at once and said without a smile, 'My friends, as Mr Chairman has gone queer, I will begin this evening with onions'. After that he went straight on with his lecture, stopping at intervals to tell us that Mr Chairman often had these little attacks, and that he had known him to go like that in the pulpit; apparently he was a sort of dissenting Minister. He then said he would show us some testing equipment with soil. He put a little earth into a glass and poured some acid onto it. The soil at once began to bubble and the old man recovering at that moment, stretched out his hand for the glass and said, 'Thank you, brother, is that scotch?' I suppose he thought it was stout, all brown at the bottom with frothy bubbles on the top; you can imagine how the audience giggled. The village lads in the front really rocked with laughter, but I thought the speaker was very bored that our attention should have been wandering from his onions to anything so unedifying. I think the Board of Agriculture ought to have an authorised list of chairmen, as well as their list of speakers.

Give Ralph much love; I hope he is all right again.

Your very loving sister

Gwendolen

*Ralph to Nita*

March 27th, 1918                           Viceroy's Camp, Dehra Dun

My own Darling,

The news from the Western Front was pretty bad yesterday, but this morning we have got a wire from the War Office which is more hopeful. It said that we had definitely driven back the enemy across the Somme, south of Peronne, and that the gap between the 3rd and 5th armies had been joined up again; still of course we have lost a very great deal of ground, especially N.W. of Peronne and S.W. of St Quentin.

Yesterday HE went fishing and caught one fish of nine lbs. which pleased him. It was rather funny how sick the Secretary of State was with him for going out for a whole afternoon and evening fishing, when he himself has been away for so many weekends! His one idea now is to get the job done, and as soon as it is done he wants to start for Bombay, but I do not think he will leave here till the 10th at the earliest now.

*Later, 3 p.m.*

A wire from the War Office puts our casualties at 75,000 and adds that the Germans claim 600 guns and 300 machine guns, which is probably correct. The wire says that the German casualties were much heavier, but gives no figures. The position on the Somme is all right for the present, but the Germans are still advancing against the French at Nesle and Roye S.E. of St. Quentin. The wire adds also that the enemy are 'very tired'; taking both our own and the enemy casualties at 150,000 and they must be more than that, it means that 2,000 men were knocked out every hour; it really is awful to think of.

Her Ex. put her large foot in it again this morning properly. She asked a Mrs Gale to come out sketching with her and said nothing to us about it but just ordered the motor for 9.45 a.m. The car was there, but Her Ex. went on reading the papers and Reuters. Johns came up to Alexander and asked him to come out and see the lady who had been standing in the road outside the gate, and who said she had an appointment with Her Ex. This was at 10.10 a.m. and turned out to be Mrs Gale who had been told by Her Ex. to be at the gate by 9.45 and Her Ex. would pick her up. She had been standing in the road for nearly twenty minutes, in front of the Native Guard, and simply burst into tears when Alexander got her inside the gate.

I really think Her Ex. is the most thoughtless, and the rudest woman sometimes I have ever met in my life. I tackled her about it after lunch and Her Ex. only said that she was sorry about it but thought I must be mistaken, as she was sure she did not leave later than 9.50 a.m.

Your own

Ralph

March 31st, 1918                    Viceroy's Camp, Dehra Dun

My own Darling,

I played golf again yesterday, and was beaten again at chess after dinner; the Secretary of State only comes into my room and watches the game, which rather puts me off! Many thanks for the Australian Mail. I have not read it yet as I have only just got back from church. What do you think the collection was for this morning? In aid of the mission to convert the Jews!! I caught HE's eye in church, I hope eight annas and my rupee will partly convert Kirsh, and the remainder help Montagu to embrace Christianity!

*Later:*

I must stop and leave this for the post as I am taking the Secretary of State out to Ambari to join HE fishing. He ought to have gone out early this morning with HE but was not well. I cannot let him go roaming over the countryside by himself, and he will not take an ADC so I am going myself with him.

Yours

Ralph

March 31st, 1918                    Viceroy's Camp, India
                                    Dehra Dun

My own Darling,

I had a long day out with the Secretary of State. We left here at 12 o'clock and first went to Col. Rennie's house at Ambari, about twenty-eight miles away. We found he was out fishing with HE so we went on and found them having lunch by the side of the river.*

It really was awfully funny to see the way HE's face fell at the sight of us; it was what I call a true fisherman's welcome! However we did not express any desire to fish and as HE and Maffey had arranged to go on to another place about twelve miles away, those two started off. We went back to Col. Rennie's house and had tea about 4 p.m. HE caught nothing in the morning and only two or three small fish in the afternoon.

I had a long and rather interesting talk to Montagu, going out in the motor. He first of all gave me his impression of the family and said that he was very fond of HE and got on very well indeed with him personally, but he said he had never met anybody like him before – quite perfectly charming in many, many ways but at the same time certain little weaknesses which one would not expect to find in him. He said that Her Ex. and also the girls, struck him as quite frankly bored with their whole existence, and consequently had the effect of boring him and the rest of them, to distraction. He said it was entirely their own fault, as he could hardly imagine any more delightful and interesting position for young girls of their age than to be the daughters of the Viceroy of India.

We then had a long talk about the political department in India and the native state side of it out here; curiously enough he said 'I think the present system of appointing young men to these political posts from the ICS is quite wrong; if I was the Viceroy I should appoint men from any walk of life purely on their suitability for these political jobs, and should choose men of usually between thirty-five and forty-five years of age, with a good general knowledge of life. I think, my dear Verney, you would make an ideal political officer, if you will allow me to say so'!! So apparently you and he are agreed that I have mistaken my profession.

Your own

Ralph

*Colonel Samuel James Rennie served with the RAMC under the Government of India as Senior Medical Officer, Delhi, 1915–19.

April 3rd, 1918                                    Viceroy's Camp, India
                                                              Dehra Dun

My own Darling

Yesterday we got out here about 5.30; Cuffs and I went for a climb and I got to the top of a high place at the back of this house and had a most glorious view right over the plain and over all the jungle here. I really must bring you out to this place some day, even if it is only for the day.

I was talking to Montagu today about our inventions, such as the tanks in connection with this War. He was awfully interesting about it. He said we invented far more things than we ever got credit for, but we are so supremely foolish in giving them away, or rather in allowing the enemy to find out about them. He was Minister of Munitions when the tank was invented and he said that everybody who had any influence, including the French Minister of Munitions, implored Haig to hold these tanks up and not to use them until at least 2,000 were available on the Western front. Montagu said that no sooner had 100 been sent over to France than Haig sent the whole lot into action; they were a huge success but very soon one was captured and the secret which nobody else but ourselves had ever thought of was given away, and the whole element of surprise done away with. Montagu is firmly convinced that if Haig had consented to wait till 2,000 tanks went into action together, it might have made the whole difference to this War.

Another thing we invented, and practically gave away, was a type of seaplane which fires torpedoes. The first one was made apparently about two and a half years ago. Instead of waiting till we had a fleet of these things ready, we sent the very first one off straight to the Dardanelles in order to destroy some useless old Turkish ships; unfortunately this one was hit and captured and in a few weeks the Germans were turning them out, the whole engine having been sent straight off to Berlin.

About the tanks, Montagu said that of every 100 tanks made, he gave one to the department called the Anti-Tank department whose object was to destroy these tanks, if the Germans had made them. So every hundredth tank which was produced was handed over to them simply for destruction and for experimental purposes, such as testing what shells or bullets would penetrate through their armour, etc.

We also invented a special kind of aeroplane which mounted infinitely faster into the air than anything produced before. The very first one that was made was sent over to France with a pilot who had never driven a single aeroplane alone in his life. He plopped down straight into a German aerodrome and of course the secret of this particular machine was given away to the enemy immediately.

What a lot a man in his position, or rather in the positions he has held, knows, about which the ordinary individual is absolutely ignorant. I think he is a most awfully interesting man once he gets talking, but it isn't so jolly easy to get him started.

Your own

Ralph

April 9th, 1918                                      Dehra Dun

My own Darling,

Montagu has taken to calling me Ralph. When he was at Mohand that night we were talking about ages, he was perfectly astonished to hear I was only three months younger than himself. He said 'you're the most wonderful person, I have never yet seen you flurried or flustered, and I have never yet known a single thing to go wrong which has been managed by you, nor have I known you to forget a single thing which you have been asked to do, even in a most casual way.' So I seem to have made an impression on the Rt. Hon. Gentleman! I got him to be quite keen on chess; we played together at Mohund and I have just got a pencilled note from him 'shall we play chess in your room after dinner?'

He is a curious mixture of a man, I really like him awfully now and understand his little peculiars, though with no side at all, yet in some little ways he is awfully touchy. The other evening, when he was watching a game of chess in my room before I went out to Mohund, he wrote HE a note saying as the report had come back from the printers, he would not be able to go out shooting as had been arranged, but there was nothing to stop the Viceroy going. He was really very offended because HE did not answer this little note himself but sent a note back to him through Maffey, saying that he would not be going out either; when I showed this to Montagu who was still in my room, he said 'I really think the Viceroy might have had the courtesy to write to me a note as I wrote to him'!

Your own

Ralph

April 10th, 1918                          Viceroy's Camp, Dehra Dun

My own Darling,

I have had a great rush of things to do last night, after dinner. HE and the Secretary of State were discussing their plans and suddenly came to the conclusion that they would go up to Simla on Saturday next, in order to have two last conferences with the executive council. So HE with P.S.V., M.S.V., Surgeon, Bunting and Montagu with all his party, except Donoughmore, are all off to Simla at 10.30 p.m. on Saturday next.

The Secretary of State will leave Simla on Wednesday evening about 10 p.m. and we shall be passing through Delhi about 6.30 a.m. on Thursday morning next week, that is the 18th. We shall not leave Kalka till 2 a.m. Her Ex. and the girls will come up on the 19th, with Alexander and Denny. I have had to fix up fresh railway programmes and many other things, but everything is now arranged.

Montagu will leave Bombay about 4 p.m. on Friday the 19th, and I am trying to arrange that we get to Bombay about 12 noon. Tell Biffy these plans; I think I may say that they are pretty fixed now, and there will not be any alterations if it can possibly be helped.

HE and Montagu have been working the whole day long lately, at this beastly report, from 10 a.m. till 7 p.m. and sometimes later than that, with just an interval for lunch and tea. They will have finished the revision perhaps by tomorrow evening, and then while it is being reprinted HE hopes to go out to Rampur Mundi with Lowndes, who arrived today, and Maffey to fish. The Secretary of State may possibly go out to Mohand, and if he decides to do this by motor just for the day, I will try and go with him.*

Her Ex. was very cross at breakfast this morning about something or other, and she happened to say that it was possible that Anne might be coming back here for this next Friday and Saturday. So I said that I had not heard of that possibility, and had put Sir G. Lowndes in her room which was the only place I could put him in, and asked if she was coming back, to which Her Ex. replied in a fretful voice that it was not very extraordinary if one of her daughters did not like to leave her for quite so long, but of course they must do whatever I decided was best!! On which HE turned on her and said that she really was at times most intransigent!!!

Your own

Ralph

*Sir George Lowndes (1862–1943) was Legal Member of the Viceroy of India's Executive Council.

April 11th, 1918                    Viceroy's Camp, Dehra Dun

My own Darling,

I am awfully depressed today to see in Reuters that all the part of the line where I was in France has been captured by the Germans, including Lanentie, where Boy Harman is buried. Fanquissart and all those trenches have been taken; they were held by the Portuguese! I feel I know every inch of that ground and can explore it so well – all our old billets now occupied by the Germans, and Estaires being easily shelled. That convent where I used to go about once a month for a hot bath, and that house which was occupied by that delightful old French lady in Estaires.

I have got such a stupid letter from that little pipsqueak Greenway, written during this trip they are taking up the gulf. He strongly objects to officers dining at Government House in Bombay in white Mess kit, no matter how hot it is, and asks me to write and say that I agree with him; he wants them to wear cloth Mess Dress always. I am afraid I wrote back very straight to him to say that the Viceroy would never think of objecting to officers dining with him in white Mess Dress in the hot weather, and that he would be quite wrong in making any such objection in view of the fact that white Mess Dress is the regulation uniform for officers to wear in certain places, and at certain times of the year in India. I also added that quite apart from this fact the Viceroy would never think of inflicting such acute discomfort on his guests by asking them to wear cloth Mess Uniform when dining with him in the middle of an Indian summer in the plains, and I quoted Madras where all officers wear white practically all the year round. I suggested to Greenway that the wearing of cloth Mess Uniform in the very hot weather would not only be extremely uncomfortable but a possible danger to certain corpulent senior officers I could mention, and might lead to an apoplectic fit at the dinner table!! Fancy a Military Secretary making such a nonsensical suggestion!

Your own

Ralph

# CHAPTER SEVEN

In April 1918 the first proof of Montagu's report arrives, but while discussing it with the Viceroy, life continues at Dehra Dun with golf, shooting and fishing when possible. By April 21st the report is completed, and Ralph accompanies Montagu's party back to Bombay for their return to England. Then Ralph goes back to Delhi, where the Viceroy is conferring with the Indian Princes.

Up in Simla on May 31st, I appear on the scene. At the end of July the Viceroy visits Bhopal, Lahore and Dhar, and back to Indore. In September Ralph returns to Simla to pack up the house and return to Delhi while Nita takes her family on a trip to Kashmir, and the Viceroy takes a holiday elsewhere in Kashmir.

*Ralph to his mother*

April 21st, 1918                                    Viceregal Lodge, Simla

My dearest Mother,

I take this last opportunity of sending a letter home by the Secretary of State's party; we leave here tomorrow afternoon and I go with them to Bombay. It will be a frightfully hot journey. I shall have one night in Bombay and then I come back to Delhi to meet the Viceroy there, on Saturday morning. He has called together a large conference of Indian Princes and other leading people, to consider how best India may respond to Lloyd George's great appeal in connection with the War. It ought to be a most interesting conference and HE is sure to make a very strong speech.

We have had to refurnish Viceregal Lodge, and all the staff houses again, in order to put up guests. It had only just been packed up and all the furniture, etc., stored in go-downs. I am sending the comptroller and a staff or servants there on Thursday, to get the place and the meals ready for Saturday morning. It will be jolly hot there, but we are only here from Saturday morning till Monday night!

I have offered, on HE's behalf, his Body Guard and his Band for service to the military authorities. The former are being turned into a training squadron under the GOC Meirut, and the latter are being formed into a platoon in the Indian Defence Force, but will remain in Simla so that the Viceroy can still have their services. I have had a very busy week making all these arrangements, and getting through a whole lot of other work before my departure tomorrow.

Capt. Holland Hibbert joins us on our way through Delhi at 1.50 a.m. on Tuesday morning! I do hope you will like him when he is at home. I have already given you his address: Munden, Watford.

Nita has really been a mother to him for the last two years!! I only hope I shall get him back again in October.

Your very affectionate.

Ralph

*Ralph to Nita*

April 27th, 1918                                    Viceroy's Camp, India
                                                             Delhi

My own Darling,

I got back here last night rather late about 9.30 p.m. after a pretty hot journey. I travelled up in the carriage with Cadell from Bombay, who is one of the representatives at this conference.[1]

Most of the chiefs coming to stay arrived very late. Carnegie spent most of yesterday at the station, and was there very early again this morning. Baroda upset all our calculations by wiring that he was making his own arrangements in Delhi, and then telephoning at 10.30 p.m. last night while I was sitting out on the lawn with John, saying that he had brought no servants with him, no motor, etc., and was expecting to come to V.R. Lodge. We sent off the wretched Carnegie with the motor at once, and fetched him along to the Mackenzie's bungalow where he is now. The first thing he asked was that he should have all his meals over there, but was told that that was quite impossible. However he was quite cheery about it.[2]

I am back from the conference which, to our astonishment, lasted only three-quarters of an hour. HE made a really excellent speech and the conference then split up into two large committees which will sit all today and tomorrow, and the whole conference assembles again on Monday at 10.30 a.m. It was a wonderful gathering of perhaps 200 men. Everybody was quite enthusiastic about HE's speech, which lasted about half an hour.

Your own

Ralph

[1] I. Sir Patrick Robert Cadell (1871–1961)
[2] Lord Carnegie was ADC to the Viceroy 1917–19. In 1923 he married HH Princess Maud, younger daughter of the Princess Royal. In 1941 he succeeded his father as 11th Earl of Southesk.

*Ralph to his mother*

May 31st, 1918                                   Viceregal Lodge, Simla

My dearest Mother,

The baby made its appearance at 2.36 a.m. this morning. Nita of course managed it that I should know nothing at all about it till it was all over. I was rather tired last night and went to bed about 10.15 p.m. She came to say good night to me at 10.45 p.m. and apparently the first signs came on about 11.15 p.m. She called Miss Wyatt who was just going to bed next door. They both fetched Shaw to help to get the cot, etc., ready, came downstairs and telephoned for Sir James Roberts as our own Col. Austen-Smith is ill with dystentry, and also telephoned for Major Robertson, our assistant surgeon.[1]

I woke up for some reason about 2.30 a.m., lit my lamp, looked at the time and listened for any noise, but hearing nothing turned out my lamp and went to sleep again. I was woken up by both doctors coming into my room before 2.50 a.m. I jumped out of bed and asked if things had started yet, only to be told it was all over and that I had a very fine son. I saw Nita myself at 3 o'clock, and I never saw her looking better in my life and most awfully pleased with herself because I had known nothing about it.

The baby weighs eight lbs. and is as ugly as it pretty well could be, but I am told there is every hope of its improving in looks as it grows older!! I went up to Nita again soon after 7 a.m. and I arranged to bring in the children about 8 a.m. They knew nothing at all about it. I fetched them myself from the nursery and told them that Mummy had something to show them, but as she had a headache they were not allowed to make a noise. They both tiptoed in and found Nita in bed with the baby.[2]

John asked if it was for him, and we told him it was a baby brother for him; on which he said 'what a delightful surprise; I will take it straight to the nursery to show Nanny!' However Nanny was called in to see it here. John then told her that when it got as big as Gervis Sleigh, who is a friend of his, he will be able to fight it!!

It is now only 10.30 a.m. but the news seems to have got all over Simla as people keep ringing me up on the telephone with congratulations. The children and Nurse came up to stay here this morning.

Nita tells me she could not help laughing at the way all our servants got up and put on their best uniform and stood about ready for the news; she looked out of my dressing-room window about 1 a.m. and saw the dhobi's wife spending the time doing some more washing. When I came out of my room with the doctors, just before 3 a.m., all the servants seemed to be collected in the hall. It was wonderfully quick, the whole thing only three hours. Nita's only complaint was that they would not give her enough chloroform; however she is most awfully well and insisted in giving me all kinds of instructions about the cable home to you; that I was to be careful, this time, about the sex and the date, etc.

I shall see her again at lunch time, and I hope she will have got to sleep. The Mail goes out this afternoon, so I can just catch it. Biffy [Holland-Hibbert] and Walter Buchanan-Riddell are to be godfathers I believe; I am told the name is to be David, but I am really not quite sure yet – perhaps I shall know more after lunch!! I will write a line later, but want to post this at once so as to make sure of catching the Mail.

Very much love, Your affectionate son

Ralph

[1]Lt-Col. Sir James Reid Roberts (1861–1941) had been Surgeon to the Viceroy 1912–16.
[2]I cannot resist a photo of myself taken a year or two later!


July 15th, 1918                      Viceregal Lodge, Simla

My dearest Mother,

The great Chelmsford-Montagu Report is now published and on the whole has been very well received in India, and also in England. I have not read it all throughout but think it very well written, and much more interesting than most reports of its kind as it gives one the whole history of how the present form of Government in India has grown up, as well as the proposals for the future.

We have got about 550 people coming here on Friday night for a concert, and next week we have an investiture to which about the same number have been invited. Except for dinner parties, of which there have been a great number this year, these are the only functions we shall have had so far.

Much love,<br>
Your very affectionate<br>
Ralph

*Ralph to Nita*

July 31st, 1918                                    Lall Kothi, Bhopal

My own Darling,

We went to the palace for a return visit this morning; it is quite an imposing place. Imagine my feeling this morning in the train, when I got a note from Alexander, about an hour before reaching Bhopal, saying he was very sorry but he had not got any red plumes with him, nor had he brought his medals with him and also was he to wear a black band round his arm?!!! I sent him back a note to say that as he had not chosen to provide himself with the proper uniform, he was not to appear the whole morning and that Cuffs would take his place in the motor cars and in the procession, etc.; that as regards his second question, it was nothing less than rank stupidity. I was too busy to see him till just before lunch when I sent for him and told him very plainly what I thought of him. Although the orders about uniform were sent round by me for this tour at least three weeks ago, he had absolutely forgotten to buy any plumes, and he said he never thought he would want his medals. I was d..d angry with him and I let him see it all right; just fancy having a man like that for one's senior ADC on tour; it isn't as if he was very young, or without any experience of things in general. He was frightfully apologetic I must say, but what on earth is the good of that? He has sent a telegram off to Denny to borrow his plumes.

We met Kenneth Barnes yesterday at a place called Bira, on his way up to Ambala. He was in a troop train and there were about 200 soldiers back from Mespot. going to various places on leave. HE got out of his train and went across to another platform where this troop train was, in order to talk to the men; he just walked down the train stopping at each carriage to have a little informal chat to the men there, asking them what their regiments were, where they were going to, what the food was like on the train, etc. I thought very few Viceroys would have taken the trouble to do that. Kenneth was very fit and sent many messages to you.

Holkar has absolutely refused to give way about the Maharani calling on Her Ex. Wood Bosanquet and I had a long talk about it this morning. Wood was rather in favour of sending him a direct order from the Government of India to say that the Maharani had got to call on Her Ex. I persuaded him not to do this now, rightly or wrongly, because I said that if he still refused, there would be nothing for it but to cancel the whole visit to Indore. Bosanquet is going there ahead of us and is to have another try at persuading him and is to say that if he persists in his refusal, he will not be visited again by any Viceroy. Personally I do not think he would care 2d about it, as anyhow he would not be visited again by a Viceroy for about five years. Bosanquet should have taken up a strong line with him right at the beginning when this visit was first proposed, then this bother would not have happened. I am afraid the only thing to do now, if he is still obstinate, is simply to say that the Maharani is not to appear at any function of any kind, and that she is to be kept absolutely purdah in her palace. I was however pleased to see that J.B. was inclined to take a strong line about it, and was not by any means pleased with Bosanquet about the whole thing, though I like Bosanquet very much personally.

Your own

Ralph

August 6th, 1918                    Manikbagh Palace, Indore

My own Darling,

We had a very good and cool journey here from Bhopal last night. We had to change into a narrow gauge train at Ujjain at 8 a.m. this morning. I got a very urgent letter given to me here from Bosanquet, saying that the Maharajah had been secretly warned that if he went through the city with the Viceroy in the motor from the station 'harm would come to him' and he was begged not to do so. Bosanquet had made all arrangements to send the first two cars by a different route altogether at the last minute, without anybody knowing anything about it except two or three police officers; unless he heard from me, this would be done but if I did not agree

I was to wire at once. I certainly did wire at once and said that the original programme was to be carried out. Everything went off all right and we came through the city as arranged. I did this because Bosanquet said in his letter that he could get no confirmation that things were wrong, and I put it down at once to pure funk on the Maharajah's part. When I had sent the telegram I told J.B. Wood who agreed with me. Of course I said nothing at all to HE about it and shall not do so, but I confess I was quite relieved to get to the guest house all right . . .

August 10th, 1918                               Viceroy's Camp, Dhar

My own Darling,

We were to have the official visits this afternoon at 3.30; we were all waiting ready at about 3.20 when Cuffs was sent for to see HE and came back in a few minutes with a very long face, and said the whole thing must be put off. The Viceroy has had a relapse, and I do not like his condition at all. He was absolutely all right at lunch time, and had asked me to fix up some buck shooting for him after tea; apparently he got a go of that neuralgia, took rather more aspirin than he ought to have done, and collapsed. When Cuffs saw him he was frightfully cold, but sweating and his temperature was down to 96°. You can imagine the state old Cuffs was in.

So we had to send a motor off at once to meet the Maharajah who was actually on his way, and stop him. We shall have to have these visits again on Monday or Tuesday, but could not decide on the date because it all depends on which day is auspicious, and the Maharajah's astrologers are finding it out for us now!!

HE is very much better this evening. I had a great argument with J.B. Wood yesterday; Jaipur had sent him a telegram the day before yesterday, asking permission to give breakfast to the Viceroy and all his party, at a place called Pilanda where we are going to stop for breakfast on the 19th, and he asked to be allowed to come there to meet HE. I refused this on my own, without saying anything to HE about it, because it is our rule that when he travels on his train he does so privately, and does not grant interviews, etc. Jaipur also sent a wire, much to the same extent, to J.B. who sent it over to me suggesting that Jaipur's offer should be accepted. I sent it back to J.B. saying that I had already refused it on my own; he then came over and saw HE and urged that it should be accepted on political grounds. HE came in with J. B. and asked me about it and I told him I thought it most unnecessary. However of course HE said that we were to fix it up between us, and that he thought on the whole he had better see Jaipur.

When I got back from the banquet I got a note from J.B. very nicely written, but asking me to do this and suggesting a reply. So I wrote back to him and said that I would bow to his decision this time, but only under strong protest, and that I hoped this would ease the political situation in India and make the work of the political secretary himself easier in the future, as of course I was always anxious to help him.

Your own

Ralph

August 14th, 1918                              Viceroy's Camp, Dhar

My own Darling,

We had a State Banquet last night and it went off so much better than I expected because, after dinner, the Maharajah produced his own musicians with Indian instruments. There was a most wonderful old boy on the drum who amused us all immensely. He was just like Old King Cole with a very round jolly face and so really loved beating this tomtom; he seemed to get as much noise out of it and to be able to do it just as fast as any man on an ordinary drum with two drum sticks – his fists went so fast one could hardly see them at all.

Then there was a Court poet who produced a long poem entirely printed out on a form about four feet high; he held his huge form in front of him and started spouting. After about five minutes, the Maharajah signalled for him to stop, on which he began to spout a little faster; in another minute or two the Maharajah gave more signals and the poet spouted faster than ever – the more signals that were given the faster he went, quite determined to finish the whole thing at all costs, until in the end he was spouting almost as fast as the drummer drummed! and he finished up quite breathless, but most triumphant. It really was too funny.

Then an old man, who looked for all the world like an owl in mourning, came forward, squatted on the ground and played the violin to us, accompanied by a man on the drum. He held his bow half way up, fiddled away at the very deuce of a rate, beating time with his knee on the floor. He wore spectacles, had a black tarbush on his head, and the most mournful expression I have ever seen on any human being. The accompaniment to all these various instruments was a sort of toy harmonium, one note of which was permanently held down, while the man blew some bellow things with his hands, so it rather had the effect of the continuous bass note on the bagpipes . . .

*Ralph to his mother*

September 14th, 1918                    Viceregal Lodge, Simla

My dearest Mother,

We are now very busy packing up most of this house for Delhi; the servants and luggage left for Kashmir yesterday. Nita and the children and two nurses leave on Tuesday morning for Pindi. I am sending my own car there by train from Dehra Dun, with the Viceroy's own English chauffeur who will drive them up to Srinagar and so get a knowledge of what the road is like before driving Their Ex.s up there next month. Our own Indian driver is going up with the servants by cart, and will be available there to drive them about up there. The car will be awfully useful to them as they are about two miles out of Srinagar at a place called Gupcar, where Hari Singh lives himself I believe. They will sleep three nights on the way up from Pindi at various dak bungalows, so the journey ought not to be very tiring, and in this way the two-wheeled cart which goes with them will be able to catch them up every evening, with their bedding and small luggage.

Your very affectionate

Ralph

*Ralph to Nita*

September 20th, 1918 Viceregal Lodge, Simla

My own Darling,

Last night Their Ex.s went to the theatre; poor Denny came to see me this morning in an awful stew saying that HE had d--d him like anything last night, being perfectly white with rage because he had sent Joan to the theatre in a carriage with Patiala. I told Denny I very likely should have done the same thing if I had been in his place, and that I knew of no order forbidding the daughters driving in a carriage with a Maharajah. I am going to have it out with HE tomorrow morning and tell him quite straight that if he has any complaint to make against the ADCs he must do so through me, and that I cannot undertake to keep the staff together these days if he treats them like that. Denny wanted to resign this morning, you know what a sensitive creature he is. He said he had never been spoken to like that before, and that he was not aware that he had done anything at all wrong.

It really is rather illogical that the Viceroy is bringing in this Reform scheme for giving Indians greater powers of governing their own country, and yet will not even allow his own daughter to go to the theatre in the same carriage with a Maharajah!! Also a Maharajah who has just been to England to represent the whole of India at the War Cabinet, and who is staying as a guest in his own house. I think it was Her Ex. really but HE told him with a white face that such a thing must never happen again, etc. The funny thing was that HE never said a word about it to me this morning, though he talked of the theatre and said how awfully good it had been.

Your own
Ralph

September 25th, 1918 Viceregal Lodge, Simla

My own Darling,

All goes well here but no news. Palestine is a splendid victory, in fact practically the whole of the Turkish army is wiped out except for 8,000 who are on the West bank of the Jordan. I was present part of the time in Council this morning. Shafi moved a resolution

that the Council should convey their earnest congratulations to
the C-in-C in France on the recent victories of the Allies. The
resolution was passed unanimously, everyone standing which was
rather impressive; a great many spoke on it but only short
speeches. The Chief spoke last representing the Government who
of course cordially supported the resolution.

Bikanir has just gone; he is staying at Chail for a few days on his
way back. As usual, he produced sheets of orders and notes for
me about the tour, and raised certain questions of precedence in
Bikanir. He asked that his son should take precedence of Manners
Smith in the carriage procession, and should drive sitting next
to Her Ex. I absolutely ruled this out. Holland rang me up and
discussed these sorts of things. I found him much more inclined to
be firm than J.B. Wood. I told Holland I would not agree to depart
from what was arranged as the correct procedure for last year, when
the tour had to be abandoned.

Very much love, your own

Ralph

September 26th, 1918                    Viceregal Lodge, Simla

My own Darling,

We had a final meeting of the Council today, and it went off most
successfully. The C-in-C made quite a sensation. A man called
Ironside from Calcutta, got up and complained of a certain Bill the
Chief had introduced this morning, saying that it showed a want of
trust on the part of the military authority for the European business
community in India. The Bill was to give the Government powers to
compel certain men to do important War work if necessary. He only
brought in the Bill this morning for discussion, and it would not
anyhow become law until the next session in Delhi, so everyone has
plenty of time to give any suggestions they like about it. Ironside
first of all asked why it was not made into law at once if it was
really necessary, and then complained about not being consulted
about it. The Chief got up in his bluff and bulldog way, and fairly
went for Ironside and pointed out how absolutely ridiculous it was
of Ironside first to complain of the Bill not being made into law
straight away, and then of not being consulted about it when the

27. Dam at one of the largest artificial lakes in Asia

28. The Royal Barge on lake at Rangoon. See p. 49

29. *SS Rankola*, used for the Burmese tour, 1916. See p. 51

30. The Irrawaddy river. See p. 54

31. The Governor of Burma's Escort, Government House, Rangoon. Troop of Military Police on Burmese ponies

32. Lodgings for the Viceregal party at Mandalay. Houses with plaited rush roofs

33. An oil well diver in Burma. See p. 52

34. Elephants hauling timber. See p.

very reason the Government did not propose to make it into law straight away was in order to give the business men in India six months to think it over, and make any suggestions about it they like. He got very angry about it, and about the accusations that he was trying to do anything without consulting the businessmen of the country; he said: 'we have all got the same object in view, I am sure of that – namely the successful prosecution of the War; why, therefore, should I want to do anything to upset my friends, the business men of India? I want to upset my enemies, not my friends.' After going on for some little time, he brought the house down by saying in a very loud voice, 'I'm not angry,' and then barked at them all just like an old bulldog. The whole Council rolled with laughter, including HE. The Chief was really quite top hole, he looked and spoke in such a good old hearty, bluff, straight forward manner, without the smallest attempt at rhetoric. He was loudly clapped on sitting down, and he had so evidently enjoyed himself thoroughly while speaking, even when he was angry.

There is a most secret and very important telegram in this morning, from the Secretary of State, about the formation of an Eastern command comprising perhaps Mespot., Persia and possibly Egypt and Palestine. The name of the present C-in-C is mentioned for this new command, in which case it will of course take him away from India. I read this telegram before HE came in to me this morning, and we had a long talk about it. HE is dead against it; he wants India to control Mespot. and Persia because we in India are the base of supplies for these two countries, and also because the military control is so absolutely mixed up with the foreign and political relations between India and Persia, and it also affects so very closely our relations with Afghanistan. I think there will have to be a special meeting of the defence committee on it, and I shall be interested to see what reply is sent to this suggestion of the Secretary of State. I think it would be a great blow to HE if the C-in-C were taken away now from India, they both get on so well together and know each other so well now.

Miss Anderson and Biddy are out at the Retreat. She sent me a little notice which she asked me to circulate to the staff, thanking them all for their very kind enquiries, etc., while they both have been isolated. I think it was really a leg pull, though she wrote me personally a very nice little note, thanking me for having sent her the Reuters so regularly every morning. I replied that it had taken all our reserve of optimism to tide us over the dull and dreary time of the absence, from the family circle, of herself and Biddy etc., and ended up by begging her to let me know if I could send out anything to the Retreat for her – anything from the Provost Marshal to a postage stamp!!

Your own

Ralph

September 30th, 1918                    Viceregal Lodge, Simla

My own Darling,

I found HE waiting to come in to me in quite a fuss about the Kashmir trip. There is quite a chance, though in my opinion a very small one, of the whole thing being cancelled. HE is awfully concerned about the scarcity of rice and food for the poor people in Kashmir which I have heard is very bad, and he sent a clear line wire to Bannerman to say that unless things were improved at once, and permanently, he would have to cancel his visit. Either this condition of things cannot be helped, in which case HE feels that it would be wrong for him to come up, or at any rate come up with such a large party, or else if this condition of things is owing to the supply of rice being held up by profiteers, HE refuses to go to Kashmir unless things are remedied at once. We ought to get a reply from Bannerman tonight . . .*

*Lt-Col Sir Arthur Bannerman (1866–1955) was Resident in Kashmir 1917–21. He was Political ADC to the Secretary of State for India 1921–28.

October 4th, 1918                       Viceregal Lodge, Simla

My own Darling,

You possibly saw that Frank Gull has been killed. I am so awfully sorry. Also Lord Alfred Browne, so those four children are now orphans; it is sad. I feel awfully depressed about poor Frank Gull – the regiment seems to have had a bad time, five officers killed in that one list.[1]

The dinner last night to Meyer was a great success. I do not think anybody knew about his GCIE. I kept the insignia in the ballroom, behind a curtain, and did not produce it until Holland came out and asked HE to proceed with the investiture. I sat next to Vincent at dinner and he had not any idea of it. HE made a very good speech and so did Meyer. Champagne made the whole difference to the success of the evening. I think we sat down seventy to dinner, the table spread out into the entrance to the Ballroom which we had furnished as a sitting-room with palms, etc.; it looked very well indeed.

A telegram has just come from Bannerman about the rice stock in Kashmir. Holland is discussing it now with HE but it seemed to me to be more or less satisfactory. General Skeen rang me up a few minutes ago to say a wire had come in to say that the Germans had evacuated Armentières and were retiring back, also a German wireless to say that Turkey had informed the Germans that she means to make peace right away. I only hope this is true.[2]

Very much love

Ralph

[1]Captain F.W.L. Gull, Rifle Brigade, was killed on 25 August, 1918.

Lord Alfred Browne (1878–1918), 5th son of the 5th Marquess of Sligo, was killed in action on 27 August, 1918. His wife had died 10 days earlier.

[2]General (Sir) Andrew Skeen (1873–1935) served in the 3rd Afghan War 1919; was Chief of the General Staff, India 1924–28.

*Ralph to his mother*

October 21st, 1918                     Camp in Dachigam Valley
                                                      Kashmir

My dearest Mother,

Our tour in this most lovely country has gone off very well so far; I rather think Nita has written to you about our arrival by river on the State Barge. Nita and the family were watching it from Hari Singh's house on the river bank, and I was able to wave to her and the children as we passed by on our stately progress.

I saw a certain amount of Nita and the family while I was in Srinagar but I never had very much time to myself on tour. Their little house is charming overlooking the dal lake, there are any number of canals and lakes near, and everybody goes about in a kind of canoe or punt, punted or paddled along by four men. The big canoes have many more – our State Barge had forty-three paddlers. The small ones, which only hold two, are called shikaras and you lie full length on the bottom with cushions, and an awning over your head, the men punting being in the stern; so you can imagine this form of travelling is much in request among the lads and lasses of Srinagar!

Of course we saw all the sights of Srinagar like the Shalimar gardens, etc. These are by far and away the most wonderful gardens I have ever seen; they have a big artificial river coming down the centre made into all kinds of waterfalls. In some place they make the waterfall of about twenty feet high and about thirty feet wide. Behind the water is a stone wall with little niches in it; in these niches are put masses of very bright red and yellow flowers, so that one looks at these masses of colour through the waterfall. The flowers show up just like very bright lamps. I have never seen that idea before. Often they have a double row of niches so that one gets a double view of these lights or flowers, as they seem to be glistening through the waterfall lit up by the bright sun.

The Maharajah's palace is built right on the river. After the State Banquet, which Nita is invited to, we come out on the balcony and watch fireworks on the river, which ought to be jolly. The resident in Kashmir is Col. Bannerman whom I knew two years ago in Bharatpur in Rajputana, when we were there. Nita's house is only about two miles from the Residency where we stay in Srinagar.

The whole river bank on both sides is lined with houseboats on which many people live all through the summer. In fact one old man, a Mr Kennard who has been out here on and off for the last thirty years, has made a houseboat his permanent home, winter and summer. He is very rich and he has made it a perfect palace of a houseboat, electric light, etc., and the most lovely furniture. It is an elaborate houseboat with two storeys and a sort of top summer house. Then he has another boat next to this one for his big drawing-room, another one next to that for his kitchen and servants. Of course it cannot be moved as it would be top-heavy, but he has other ones on the lakes; these he uses for shooting.

The War news is too splendid for words. I wonder how long the Germans intend to go on fighting, they must know by now they are a beaten nation.

Very much love, your very affectionate

Ralph

*Ralph to Nita*

November 11th, 1918                              Viceregal Lodge, Delhi

My own Darling,

I have had no Reuters today, but I believe the Armistice will be signed today, our wedding day – rather curious if his awful War comes to an end on our wedding day.

I have just got your dear telegram. You sent it off at just before 11 a.m. and I was reading it here in my bed at 12.10, so that was pretty quick! I shall certainly take every care while I am convalescing. I certainly hope the next nine years will be as happy and full of interest as the last nine, and that your children will increase in size but not in number!!

I keep wondering if all our troops in France have stopped fighting yet. I feel sure they must have done so. I expect there will be terrific cheering all down the lines when the order 'cease fire' is given. Cannot you imagine The Stiffen's delight – the War over and he returns a full Major-General, etc. I do feel so sorry for all those killed the last day or two.*

Your own

Ralph

*'The Stiffen', General Shute, was Ralph's Colonel in India in 1913.

*Nita to her mother*

November 1918                                    Gupkai, Srinagar

My dear Mother,

   As soon as he left Srinagar, we all went out to Islamabad and
Achebal by house-boat and motor, but I was not there very long
before I began to feel miserably depressed, and instinctively felt
Ralph was not well.* I could not bear it any longer but motored
eleven miles to the nearest post office where I wired to him and to
Mrs Mackenzie, asking her to let me know at once how he got ill. I
had not felt like it since he was in France, and was not surprised at
receiving wires in answer that he had been in bed for the last three
days with 'flu, this Spanish 'flu, but all the wires implored me not to
go down as it would take five days, and Ralph would be up and
about; I could not take the children as the house would be infec-
tious, and Ralph and the doctor felt very strongly that they should
not run any risk of catching it, it would undo all the good of the
Kashmir trip; David of course is tied to me still. Ralph since then
has wired to me daily, and is so much better he is tomorrow to meet
Harry [Verney] at Bombay; it is such a great piece of luck that he is
free to go. The Bikanir tour is off because of this flu, also Jhodpur,
for the little Maharajah there died of pneumonia. HE had to go up
to Simla instead of Delhi, for none of his government moves down.
Ralph went with Her Ex. to Delhi and says it is so hot.

         Much love, and may this Xmas be a very happy one.
                  Your affectionate daughter

                              Nita

*Not for nothing was my mother a Celt and the seventh child of a seventh child!!

# CHAPTER EIGHT

By November 11th the Viceroy is back in Delhi. Ralph goes to Bombay to meet Claydon Harry and the Viceroy's camp is back in Calcutta by December 10th for three weeks of continuous activity.

The Viceroy returns to Delhi on January 7th, 1919 for a conference of all the Governors of India, and leaves on a Spring Tour in March visiting Baroda, Hydrabad and Madras.

*Harry to Ralph's mother*

November 19th, 1918                    Government House, Bombay

My dearest Aunt Maudy,

I think you know what a thrill of joy it was to me that Ralph should be the first person I should see as the ship came alongside yesterday morning. He had come all the way from Delhi. He has had 'flu rather badly, but I must say he seemed to me to look very well.

As I watch him among the people of Bombay who all know him, I have a feeling that he MUST be the VICEROY and that a gentlemen called Lord Chelmsford is his Military Secretary. He is to the manner born; beautifully uniformed men are waiting to respond to his every whim, and as I am on speaking terms with him I, too, come in for some of his reflected glory.

We are to have over a week in India, so I am off to Delhi with him tomorrow and hope to get just a glimpse of Nita and the children.

Your very loving

Harry

*Ralph to Nita*

December 14th, 1918                    Viceroy's Camp, Calcutta

My own Darling,

I am so glad you were going to hire a car and go out to meet the aeroplane. It is due here next Tuesday afternoon at 2.30 p.m. and I suppose there will be 100,000 people to watch it arrive on the Brigade parade ground.*

We had another dinner party last night which went off all right – about fifty people altogether. Before dinner, about 7 p.m. I was sitting working in my office when Her Ex. came in and sat down and started chatting away about all sorts of things. She said how rare it was to find anybody with really what she called 'staff intuition'. I was quite touched when she said that they had never had anyone so good on their staff as myself, or anybody who was so absolutely born for the work, as she seemed to think I was. I do not know why she suddenly took the trouble to say something pleasant

like that to me, especially as I have had to tackle her again about
these garden expenses; perhaps she thinks she will twist me round
her finger by saying that, but I am not going to be taken in all the
same!

Very much love; I hope the children are all flourishing.

Ralph

*In December Major-Gen W.G.H. Salmon, DSO, accompanied by Capt. Ross
Smith arrived in a Handley Page V 1500 Bomber called HMA *Old Carthusian* in
the first flight from England to India via France and Egypt. Shortly afterwards this
was followed by a second similar aircraft which brought General McEwen and was
piloted by Major A.S. Mclaren and Capt. Halley. These aircraft were designed to
bomb Berlin but were not completed in time and so instead were flown to India to
be used successfully in bombing Kabul in the War against Afghanistan.

December 19th, 1918                    Viceroy's Camp, Calcutta

My own Darling,

Her Ex. came into my room this morning again, and had such a
long talk about the girls. She told me she had had a letter from
Sheepshanks this morning, and that Biddy thinks she wants to
marry him, but that Her Ex. is not going to allow the engagement
until they have been at home some time, and Bid has had a chance
of seeing other men. But it looks to me as if this marriage will come
off. Then she talked about Anne, and said that she did not think
Carnegie intended marrying her and asked what I thought. I told
her perfectly straight that I agreed with her, and that I did not think
he intended doing anything of the kind. I arranged with her to send
Wakeman home in March with Joan, and to send Carnegie home in
July. She talked to me about leaving Anne and Carnegie together in
Simla, and I said that she had better tell Anne herself not to
confine herself entirely to him, as it only made her conspicuous
and put other people off her. She promised to do so. I asked
whether she would like Carnegie to stay on as extra ADC and she
said she thought he had better definitely go in July or August. I
said I would tell both Wakeman and Carnegie in Delhi, about these

plans. Wakeman is about the biggest oaf I have ever seen on any staff and I shall be glad to be quit of him!!

Your own

Ralph

*Ralph to his mother*

December 28th, 1918                                   Viceroy's Camp, Calcutta

My dearest Mother,

We are in the middle of a very busy time here – during our three weeks in Calcutta we shall have had five dinner parties of about fifty, an evening party of 600, a garden party of about 3,000, a levee of about 1,400, a ladies' and purdah party, a dance and a children's party, besides attending the races in State and the 1st January Proclamation Parade, and also a visit to Cooch Behar of four days! Also a visit to a place called Sakchi which involves two nights in the train to see the Tata Iron Works. I think this may be considered a pretty full programme, and that the Viceroy may be said to have entertained pretty lavishly in Calcutta this time.

Very much love, Your very affectionate

Ralph

January 7th, 1919                                   Viceregal Lodge, Delhi

My dearest Mother,

Your telegram about the election reached us this afternoon. I am awfully sorry about Harry, but I am awfully glad about the result of the general election as a whole, which I am afraid you're not. Personally, I think Lloyd George who has done more than anyone else to win the War, should be the man to run the show – at any rate until things have settled again. In fact I should be very hard put to it to nominate any one to fill his place; apparently the majority of the country are of the same opinion, from the huge majority he has got in the new House. He has been given a magnificent opportunity and it remains to be seen what use he will make of it.*

We have got all the Governors and Lt. Governors, etc., coming here for a conference next week. Lord Pentland is about the only one not coming. After that we have got an Indian Chief's conference, so these two things will keep us busy this month. On Jan. 30th the Viceroy is going to review about 10,000 Nepalese troops in Delhi, before they return to their own country. They have been used for part of the Indian garrison during the War, and were lent to us by the ruler of Nepal. On the 24th we have a garden party here and an investiture.

Your very affectionate

Ralph

*Claydon Harry had stood as a Liberal.

February 13, 1919                                    Viceregal Lodge, Delhi

My dearest Mother,

I much hope that Francis Smith will have accepted that offer of £2,500 for No. 12 C.P. It may not seem much to you, but at the same time, it is such an expensive house to live in that I do feel strongly that we should not refuse any reasonable offer of getting rid of the house now; and with the heavy taxation which everybody will have to bear for many years to come, the number of people who can afford to live in Connaught Place will be rather limited.[1]

Lord Montagu of Beaulieu is in Delhi again; he is lunching with us today. He comes out here every winter, to advise the Government of India about Mechanical Transport, but nobody has ever discovered that he is really of any use at all; he is one of those people who seem to be able to wander about the world at their own sweet will, at the expense of a grateful British public. He wears a wound stripe for having been sunk in the *Persia*![2]

Very much love,<br>Your very affectionate

Ralph

¹Francis Smith was the family solicitor.
²The 2nd Baron Montagu of Beaulieu (1866–1929) was a pioneer of motoring.

*Nita to Ralph's mother*

February 14th, 1919                    Viceregal Lodge, Delhi

My dearest Mother,

I forgot to ask you, in the last letter I wrote, if you would be so kind as to offer the use of our stored furniture to Capt. Holland Hibbert, Herts. Yeomanry, Munden, Watford. It will save us paying £15 a year and will be of the greatest use to him and his young wife; he writes nearly every Mail how expensive it is to buy, they don't know how they are going to manage. We have just thought what a good idea it would be, as it is not good for furniture to be put away for so long. We are so fond of him, and we should like him to have it.

My best love. John is much better tonight. Your very affectionate

Nita

*Ralph to his mother*

March 13th, 1919                    Viceregal Lodge, Delhi

My dearest Mother,

I am awfully glad to hear about Harry [Lloyd Verney, a cousin,] having been made Private Secretary to the Queen. By-the-by I have been given the 3rd Class of the Order of the Sacred Treasure by the Emperor of Japan!!

Your very affectionate

Ralph

March 22nd, 1919                    Viceregal Lodge, Delhi

My dearest Mother,

We have got a pretty hot tour in front of us now, and in some ways a difficult tour from my point of view, as the three Maharajahs we are going to visit are the three most difficult ones in the whole of India. I have already had a good deal of preliminary correspondence in connection with the arrangements, and by taking up a firm attitude I hope I have guarded against any unfortunate contretemps, as far as possible.

Very much love, your very affectionate<br>Ralph

*Ralph to Nita*

March 20th, 1919            Viceroy's Camp, Baroda

My own Darling,

I think the Gaekwar has done all he could to make this visit a success and he seemed most affable and anxious to please. We had very little to do with the Maharani, though she is dining here tonight. I am sure she is the difficult one of the two.

There is an American housekeeper here who rejoices in the designation 'Director of Domestic Arts'!! Domestic Arts consists of providing us with every kind of scent and powder bottle imaginable in our rooms. We are even provided with a toothbrush, each sealed up in a little box. Face powder, nail polishers, shaving powder, eau de Cologne, etc. etc., I have never seen such a collection of toilet accessories in my life before! Even a pair of new hairbrushes each, is provided.

Very much love, my own darling, and give my love to the children.

Your own<br>Ralph

March 27th, 1919            Falaknuma Castle, Hyderabad

My own Darling,

I have been interrupted with all sorts of official visits, and seeing many people about all kinds of things. I have to go and fetch the Nizam and bring him here for his official visit to HE and then we go and return the call, officially, this afternoon. Everything is on a very much bigger scale here than in Baroda.

The Nizam has got four palaces in Hyderabad but he personally never leaves the one he lives in except, every now and then, to go and play tennis at the Residency or to pay a visit to one of his other palaces. He does absolutely nothing at all, as far as I can make out. It must be a delightful life, and of course he is most frightfully particular about etiquette and doing exactly what his father did before him, etc.

Our visit to Baroda was really a very great success and I think HE has done a lot of good by going there; he went to tea privately with the Gaekwar and the Maharani and they were both quite charming to him. She took him all round her own private rooms, showed him her clothes, etc., the only little contretemps was that both her sons got drunk on the occasion of the quiet dinner just before we left; the second son was frightfully drunk, and talked a whole lot of rot to me about Oxford and the Bullingdon of which he was NOT a member, and it was all I could do to prevent him embracing me on the platform when we parted. Of course the heir is the grandson, the son of the eldest son of the Gaekwar who died, largely from drink, I am afraid.

The Nizam has just had a private talk with HE which we expected to last at least an hour; in twenty minutes the Nizam was out again, and we had a great rush to get the guard of honour fallen in again, and to get Fraser and the other officers here to see him off, etc. etc. – he is frightfully particular about his dignity.

Those two fit sons of the Nizam were at the Banquet last night, and that little girl of his was standing behind his chair most of the time, being fed on ices!! This afternoon we were going to Secunderabad and then to a place called Bolaram where we have to have a reception of Indian officers at the Residency there.

The Residency house here in Hyderabad is a beautiful one, and the Frasers have got it filled with the most beautiful collection of things such as brass pictures, armour, shooting trophies, etc. Lady Fraser told me they will have to sell most of it as they could not possibly take it home with them. This is a very good post as far as salary goes; I think he gets 4,000 Rs. a month and also a sumptuary allowance of 1,000 Rs. a month. There is a splendid flight of marble steps leading up to the house which rather reminded me of those at Belvedere, on a smaller scale.*

By-the-by, about the Maharani of Alwar, she was the niece of the Jam Sahib who was staying here at the time that she shot herself. If he comes to Simla, I wonder if we shall get the true story of that tragedy out of him; I doubt it, as he will probably stick up for his order of Princes and will not give Alwar away. I expect Alwar is in a furious temper about HE not going there, and will vent his anger on those who were responsible for allowing her to get hold of that revolver with which she shot herself.

Your own

Ralph

*Sir Stuart Fraser was Resident at Hyderabad 1916–19.

March 29th, 1919                    Falaknuma Castle, Hyderabad

My own Darling,

Biddy is engaged to Sheeper, though I suppose it isn't actually announced yet, but HE had heard from Her Ex. that they seemed to have made up their own minds about it, so he is writing this week to Sheeper saying that he now allows the engagement.*

Yesterday afternoon, we went out through Secunderabad to Bolaram, and had a big reception of Indian officers who all passed by the Viceroy who shook hands with each of them. There was one magnificent old officer there with over fifty years' service, with a long white beard and standing over six feet – he really was the most picturesque figure I have seen in India. HE had him up afterwards and talked to him by himself.

I have just come back from seeing them all off at the station, and I am quite alone in this huge palace. This afternoon we all went out to Goloconda which is a big fort with a good many old tombs there, where we were given tea by the Nizam. After tea we were all sent off to see the tombs so as to give HE the opportunity of having a good straight talk to the Nizam. I know exactly what HE said to him because as soon as we got back here, he came into my room and repeated practically for word what he had said, referring to the notes he had made beforehand. He gave him a very straight talking to, saying, among other things, that there was one thing the Government of India could not prevent and that was private revenge – giving as an instance the assassination of the Amir.

I had a talk at Golconda to the Second Chief of Police there, and I was very astonished at some of the things he told me about the Nizam; for instance the other day, Sir Brian Egerton, who looks after some schools here, said to the Nizam in conversation, that he had had trouble with two boys whose names he gave. The Nizam sent for them, had them held down, and with his own hand gave them such a beating that one of the boys was in hospital for some weeks, and the other said he would certainly shoot the Nizam one day. Then also, if ever he gets angry with any of his women, he sends for a bundle of sticks and beats them unmercifully himself with his own hands; he has got no government at all really – he just appoints ministers to do the work, and then in a fit of temper he gives them the sack, takes away all their money or land, etc. Can you wonder he is absolutely loathed by all his people, though of course everybody is frightened to death of him.

HE told him quite straight, things could not go on like this and told him within six months he was to have a proper Government with a Prime Minister who must receive the Viceroy's approval. HE told him that he had absolutely forfeited the affection and good will of his people by his cruelty and bad temper; he also gave him the names of certain officials whose advice he was not to pay any attention to, and whom he was to have nothing to do with in future. I cannot stand the man. After dinner tonight, I happened to say to Fraser that we would all go on ahead of the Viceroy and the Nizam to the station, and be ready to receive them at the station; imagine my astonishment when Fraser said that the Nizam was not coming to the station at all, but would say goodbye to HE at his own palace where we were dining, as it was only a private departure, and that he did not go to the station to see Lord Hardinge off. I said that considering that the Viceroy had taken the trouble to travel, and to come all the way from Delhi to see the Nizam, it seemed to me monstrous that the Nizam should not come even as far as the station to see him off, and I left it at that. But the Nizam did not come. I do not think HE minded, but I confess I felt very angry.

Your own

Ralph

*Biddy married Major Richard Sheepshanks (d. 1951) in June, 1919. They were divorced in 1937.

March 31st, 1919                    Government House, Madras

My own Darling,

Before leaving Hyderabad, I asked that very nice ADC of the Nizam's if he would be kind enough to let me have a few sand-wiches, a little cake, some fruit, and a few bottles of soda-water to take with me in the train. When I got to the station, I saw a big new box with brass handles that did not belong to me at all, also two large baskets. I pointed this out to the ADC who said that they were mine, and contained my food for the train. I opened the box and found every drink there I could possibly want, including brandy, claret, champagne, cider and any amount of soda-water and Perrier!! I asked where I should send this box back to, and was told it was for me and I was not to send it back at all. In the other basket was everything from a tea-pot to a salt-cellar, and in the third basket was enough food to last me six months!! So when dinner-time came on the train, we got Lady Birkett, whom I knew in Bombay, and a Mrs Giffard, the wife of the Surgeon-General there, to come into our carriage and we gave them dinner – iced drinks, fruit cake, boiled eggs, etc. etc. I had to throw away some partridges and other meat, as the heat made them go bad in a very few hours.*

Your own

Ralph

*Lady Birkett was the wife of Sir Thomas Birkett (1871–1957), Additional Member of the Governor's Council 1915–16; Sheriff of Bombay 1917.

Mrs Giffard's husband rose to be Major-General Sir Gerald Giffard (1867–1926). He was Surgeon-General to the Government of Madras from 1919 to 1924.

April 9th, 1919                    Queen's Cottage, Newara Eliya

My own Darling,

I got a wire from the PSV to say that Her Ex. had wired out to ask HE to take on Carnegie again for five months as ADC and that HE had approved. I suppose that Her Ex. thought that this fish might wriggle off the hook again with such a long line, and that it was safer to have him within reach!! I wrote to HE last night to say that as he had decided about it I was quite ready to accept this decision, but I asked him quite definitely not to keep Carnegie on after his marriage, either as ADC or as Extra, as I thought it would not answer at all. Personally, I am awfully sick that he is coming back at all; he leaves London the beginning of May, and it is an obvious wangle on the part of Her Ex. in order that he may draw staff pay!! I lay awake last night and worried over it, which was stupid of me. Anyhow I hope it means that there can be no doubt but that the wedding will take place in October, which will be the five months asked for by Her Ex. Another ADC is coming out with him, but I told HE I supposed Her Ex. had explained to him that he could only come as extra, now that David was to return.

Maffey has also let me down over the OBE for Parsons, which I was afraid he would do all along. He wired that he could not get the decoration for him, but as he had accepted the MBE for his Registrar, he advised me to do the same for Parsons, which I have had to do, because if the PSV's man receives a decoration I certainly do not think Parsons should be left out. But I wrote to HE about this, also giving him my views in case Maffey had not done so, and I quoted Francy's OBE and I said that Parsons deserved equal recognition at least, both on account of his work for the last five years and also on account of his status as a gazetted officer. I wrote a straight letter to Maffey about it, and then tore it up next morning on second thoughts!! But I am very disappointed about it, and I feel that there are two things that have happened since I have been away which I would have tried to prevent. However it is no good worrying and I suppose HE has a perfect right to alter his mind and have David back if he likes; but I shall not stay on as MSV if he wishes to have him after he is married. I would much sooner chuck it.

Your own

Ralph

# CHAPTER NINE

In June, Her Excellency returns to England for Bridget's wedding but is back in time for their own silver wedding on July 27th. The Amir of Afghanistan comes to Rawal Pindi to discuss peace. The Viceroy takes the opportunity to visit the N.W. Frontier but returns to Simla by September 20th for a large Investiture and Legislative Council meeting, finishing with a State Ball.

By October 20th the Viceroy is on tour again, visiting Patiala, having lunch with the Maharajah of Jindi, tea at Maler Kotla and the night at Nabbha, before returning to Dehra Dun. On November 3rd the Viceroy opened the newly constituted Chief's Conference in Delhi and on the 21st started off on yet another tour, this time to Madras, then on to Bangalore and Mysore, then to a Keddah camp where they saw wild elephants being coralled and back to Mysore, finally ending up in Calcutta on December 17th.

*Ralph to his mother*

June 18th, 1919                                    Viceregal Lodge, Simla

My dearest Mother,

I am glad to say the Amir has accepted our armistice terms and
the negotiations for peace will begin in Pindi at the beginning of
next month; should these fail, which I think very unlikely, we shall
by that time be in a very strong position, especially with regard to
aeroplanes, and should have enough to begin an offensive at any
moment and should be able to blow Kabul sky high, if necessary.
However I do not think for a moment there is any chance of active
operations beginning again. I am sorry to say Dick Ridgway got a
slight heat stroke and had to be sent away from the Khyber; he is
now in Murree, I am so sorry for him because his brigade has now
been given to some one else, a General Sheppard, and one does not
know if he will be given another one when he is well enough. But
still, I hope he may get another one later on.[1]

I hope to take HE down to Poona for a few days next month, and
meet Her Ex. in Bombay and bring her back; this will make a nice
break in the Simla time for HE, and he will also very much enjoy
spending two or three days with the Lloyds at Poona, both of whom
he likes immensely. We shall leave here about July 11th, and get
back again about the 20th.[2]

Their Silver Wedding is on the 27th when I think we shall just
have a staff dinner here and give them a big silver salver, with all
our autographs engraved on it, which Denny is bringing out with
him from home, and on Monday the 28th we have a silver wedding
ball here for about 500 people.

Our plans for the autumn are taking shape; we are going on an
official visit to Patiala about October 20th, then go to Dehra Dun
for five or six days and then we start off on our Southern India
tour on November 22nd, visiting Mysore, Bangalore, Madras, etc.,
getting to Calcutta on Dec. 15th where we shall be for three weeks
or so, and visit Benares on our way back to Delhi, which we shall
not reach till about Jan. 15th. We are going to have a Keddar
in Mysore, which will be most interesting. A Keddar is a wild
elephant hunt and takes some weeks to do, but we only see the
last few days of it by which time all the wild elephants which
may number nearly 100, have been slowly driven towards the big

stockades which have been built to catch them in. The wild ones are driven along, I believe, by tame ones, and it requires much skill as well as much pluck, to manoeuvre these wild ones into the stockade. We shall be in camp for about ten days nearly, and shall hope to get some shooting as well.

Your very affectionate son

Ralph

[1]Brigadier-General Richard Ridgway (1868–1939) served in the Afghan Campaign of 1919, sometimes called the 3rd Afghan War.
  Major-General Seymour Sheppard (1869–1957)
[2]George Ambrose Lloyd, 1st Baron Lloyd (1879–1941) was Governor of Bombay 1918–23. In 1925 he was appointed High Commissioner for Egypt and the Sudan. He married (1911) Blanche, sister of Alan Lascelles.

June 26th, 1919                                     Viceregal Lodge, Simla

My dearest Mother,
  The other evening, Nita and I went to dine with the C-in-C and Lady Monro, for the presentation of these Japanese decorations. The Chief himself got the Rising Sun, General Sir George Kirkpatrick and myself got the order of the Sacred Treasure, General Scott got the 2nd Class of the Rising Sun, and Mrs Skeen got the Japanese order, on behalf of her husband who is on service. The little ceremony took place after dinner in the big drawing-room, and the Japanese Consul-General invested us with these decorations in the name of the Emperor of Japan. The Chief made a very nice little speech on behalf of us all, and talked about the Japanese and the British Arms in the future marching along side by side in the cause of Peace and progress, etc. etc.; nothing very original, but still he said it very nicely and he looked the part of a British Commander-in-Chief so admirably.*
  I must tell you of a delightful remark of John's yesterday. He came with me into my dressing-room yesterday evening and my bearer had just put this new medal ribbon on my uniform coats and John, who had admired the whole decoration very much, asked to be shown which the ribbon was. He said 'I do not quite understand

why you have got this medal, because you have not done any very brave act just lately, have you Daddy?'!!! I love the 'just lately'!

There is one thing I wonder if you would be willing to do for the John Mackenzies? You know he is the Comptroller here, and is a most charming person and has worked most loyally under me. Will you allow him to go for a bit, when he arrives home, to the flat – he and his wife and his little girl of about two and a half with perhaps a nursery maid. They are not at all well off, and I know he will be immensely grateful. He leaves Bombay on Sept. 6th, so would be home by about the end of that month. Perhaps you will be using it at that time, or may have lent it to somebody else; in which case do not bother about it . . .

*General Sir George Kirkpatrick (1866–1950) was Chief of the General Staff, India 1916–20.

Major-General Sir Arthur Scott (1862–1944) commanded Lucknow Division, India 1918–20

July 23rd, 1919                              Viceregal Lodge, Simla

My dearest Mother,

We had a charming visit to the Lloyds at Poona, or rather at Ganneshkhind which is their Government House about four miles out of Poona.

We had three days there this time, and then went to Bombay where we met Her Ex. on Thursday morning. We went down to the ship and found her very well, but having had a really hot journey out. Capt. Denny and the two new ADCs were on board. We left Anne Thesiger in Bombay, and she sailed for home on Saturday. Her engagement to Lord Carnegie is broken off; she is going home for about four months and will return with John Mackenzie in December.[1]

Denny brought out with him the staff present to Their Ex.s for their Silver Wedding, which is next Sunday. We are going to have a staff dinner party and I shall have to make a short speech and present it, as Maffey is away. Hignell, who is now Private Secretary, said he would rather I did it as I have been so long on the staff, so I shall have to think of something to say. It is a silver salver with their crest in the centre and a small inscription, and all our signatures engraved on it – twenty-one in all, including wives, and Miss Anderson, who has been living with us for over two years, and is being considered a sort of lady-in-waiting. It is only the staff actually serving now with the Body Guard officers.[2]

I have, at the present moment, got no less than seven ADCs under me though our senior ADC, Major Alexander, is leaving us in about another month or so.

Very much love, your very affectionate

Ralph

[1]Lt. Colonel John Mackenzie (1876–1949) had been Comptroller of the Household under the Earl of Minto 1907–10 and Lord Hardinge 1910–16. He held the same post under Lord Chelmsford 1916–21 and was Military Secretary to the Earl of Lytton, Governor of Bombay, 1922–27.
[2]Sidney Robert Hignell (1873–1939) was the Viceroy's Private Secretary from 1919 to 1924.

*Ralph to Nita's father*

July 24th, 1919                                    Viceregal Lodge, Simla

My dear Daddy,

To turn for a moment to more serious matters, the delegates from the Amir of Afghanistan reached our frontier posts this morning at 11 a.m. and are now on their way to Rawal Pindi to discuss terms of peace. Our representatives are already there, and I much hope that in two months from now peace will have been arranged and that our much tried troops, who have been living in a temperature of 120 in the shade largely in tents, may be safely withdrawn from the frontier to more attractive stations with proper barracks; also a large proportion of them are temporary soldiers, waiting to be sent back to England on demobilization, which had to be suspended in this country until all danger of a large Frontier Campaign was over. Some of them found it difficult to appreciate the reasons for their retention in India.

Your affectionate son

Ralph

*Ralph to Nita*

August 14th, 1919, 4 p.m.                    Viceroy's Camp, India

My own Darling,

We have had a most awfully interesting morning starting at 7 a.m. We really inspected the Brigade which Dick had in camp, this side of Jamrud, and now commanded by General Shepperd who showed us all over his camp and his brigade; then we motored on to Jamrud where we had breakfast with General Christian and his staff. Sir Arthur Barrett, General Sir Charles Dobell and R. Kappell all came with us. After breakfast we must have spent nearly three hours inspecting the whole of the Jamrud brigade.*

The whole place looks so different to what it does in ordinary times. New roads are being built, a rope railway is being put up through the pass, masses of troops and transports are everywhere, and huge camp all round Jamrud, on the way to which we climbed up to Fort Mandi where on July 18th there was a big fight against about 400 to 500 Afghans, and one of our picquets was cut off. An officer called Oates was in command, and it was he who commanded this post in that fight. He is an Australian from Ballarat and knows Trawalla and the Bridges; he is going to stick to the Indian Army.

Now, in half an hour, we are off to Nowshera; we are going to Dakka on Wednesday, then go by train that night to Kohat. On Thursday, we inspect Hungu Thal and go right through to Parachinar, where we spend Friday. We return Friday morning, by motor to Kohat, and entrain again at 2.30 p.m. for Pindi and Simla. We saw Maffey and Grant who lunched with us just the other side of Pindi, both very well and happy. It is pretty stuffy here in Peshawar, but it was not really too hot up in the Khyber this morning, so long as one did not stop inside a tent.

We are escorted by armoured cars, besides another car with some men with loaded rifles. I have been kept very busy indeed so far, arranging programmes, inspections, etc.

Yours

Ralph

*Brigadier-General Gerard Christian (1867–1930)

General Sir Arthur Barrett (1857–1926) was commander of Northern Command, India 1916–20. In 1921 he was made a Field-Marshal.

Lt.-General Sir Charles Dobell (1869–1954) commanded a Division in the Third Afghan War.

*Ralph to his mother*

September 20th, 1919            Viceregal Lodge, Simla

My dearest Mother,

We have had a very busy week with three rather large functions; a dance on the 12th, a concert on the 15th and a large investiture on the 17th, at each of which entertainments there were over 300 people present.

The Investiture was really a great success; we all wore Full Dress and HE wore his Star of India robes. I had a good many of the Body Guard posted about to add to the general effect, and I also had six scarlet-coated mace bearers leading the procession into the Ballroom, right up the whole length of the dining-room. These six mace bearers were followed by eight of the staff in full dress, then came Their Ex's followed by two pages, the sons of two ruling chiefs, holding up HE's robes. After Their Ex's had taken up their position under a big red and gold canopy, the mace bearers and the staff filed to the right and left, and stood on each side.

The investiture of ninety-nine decorees then began. We had about six or eight knights to dub, when they kneel on a stool in front of HE to whom I handed my sword. After the investiture was over we processed out again, the Band playing, of course, the National Anthem, and then we all had refreshments in the big drawing-room to the strain of more lively music.

We have not got another big show now till Oct. 3rd, which is the State Ball at which about 1,000 will be present, and for this we have already put up large shamianas which have got to be properly lined with scarlet cloth, etc. Of course this is the first summer we have really gone in for entertaining on a big scale, but I rather doubt if any previous Viceroy has done so much entertaining as HE has done up in Simla this summer. Full Dress will be worn again for this State Ball, and the Lloyds from Bombay will be staying for it.

We have been having the Legislative Council meetings, and yesterday was a most interesting day when they passed the

Indemnity Bill through its first stages. This is a Bill to indemnify all officers and men for any action done in good faith, during the period of Martial Law in the Punjab last April, May and June.

The Council sat from 11 a.m. to 8 p.m. with an interval of one hour for lunch. I was there the whole time, and it was certainly the best debate I have yet heard in the Council. There had been great opposition to this Bill by a certain number of the Indian members, but the Government members had the best of the argument the whole way through, especially Sir George Lowndes, the life member, who spoke splendidly for over an hour towards the end. I am really very keen about these Council meetings although, of course, they do not really concern me at all, but HE and I usually discuss next morning what has happened the previous day. We have got a Council dinner on Thursday this week to which most of them come; it means a dinner of about sixty altogether, with the staff.

Your very affectionate son

Ralph

October 9th, 1919                    Viceregal Lodge, Simla

My dearest Mother,

Our State Ball went off quite well last Friday. Sir George and Lady Lloyd from Bombay arrived that morning; I like them both so much – they have now gone on to Kashmir. We ended up our entertainments here, for the Season, with a children's party here yesterday – about 240 mothers, nurses and children.

Maffey, our Private Secretary, is resigning and is going home next March and is being succeeded by a charming man called Hignell whom I like immensely, and who has been acting Private Secretary for the last four months. I am really delighted that Mrs Maffey is going. I have never cared for her at all, and my biggest feather in my Military Secretary's cap will ever be that I have lived in close proximity to that woman for nearly four years without having a serious row with her!! So I am really glad that Maffey is going, and that Hignell is taking his place in March.

We have been having trouble on the Waziristan frontier, and I am much afraid we shall have to have an expedition against these tribes before long. We are going to see what we can do with aeroplanes first, in order to bring them to their senses. We are so busy in India with demobilisation and the arrival of fresh troops from England, that we are not anxious to embark on another Frontier War just now.

Very much love, your very affectionate

Ralph

*Ralph to Nita*

October 21st, 1919                    Baradari Palace, Patiala

My own Darling,

I have just come back from fishing again, but this evening I went to a different tank to HE. I got a really big fish weighing 19 pounds; he took me 25 minutes to land. HE in his tank caught 2 fish, one 13 lbs and the other about 10 lbs.

This afternoon, we had the unveiling of that statue to King Edward. We had to put on Full Dress Uniforms for it, and the whole ceremony only lasted five minutes.

This morning we visited schools and the hospital, and also we went to see some Indian wrestling; great fat men struggled on the ground in a circle made of sand, and when they got hot, which they jolly soon did, they got covered in this sand which turned into mud. It was not a particularly edifying sight, but still rather interesting to see. I lunched with the Maharajah at his own Palace, just Maffey and myself, and we had a ten course lunch – needless to say, I passed about eight out of the ten courses.

Her Ex. is dotty on sketching, and goes out with an ADC whenever she can get away. We are going out for a shoot tomorrow morning on elephants; pig and partridges are to be the bag. I shall try and go fishing again in the evening.

Very much love, yours

Ralph

October 24th, 1919                                     Dehra Dun

My own Darling,

We had a large State Banquet last night at Patiala, but my next
door neighbour refused course after course; a very shy old man
whom I had not met before. I said to him that I was afraid he
did not seem to be very hungry; he answered that he was sorry, but
he had got something or other which I could not quite catch,
but I thought it was some kind of disease which prevented him
eating, but further enquiries made it clear that what he had got
was 'scruples'; he meant that he had scruples about feeding with
Europeans, so he dined on a glass of soda-water.

At Nabbha, the next night, at dinner there I sat next to a very old
man indeed, who had Holland the other side of him. I made some
futile remark about the band or something, just to open negotiations with him, but he took no notice at all, so I dug him in the
ribs and repeated my futile remarks only to find that he was
absolutely stone deaf, and could not think why I had been so
familiar as to dig him in the ribs! I watched Holland trying to open
conversation with him, and nearly split myself with laughing at his
equally futile attempts. The Nabbha Sirdars seemed to be all of
them over eighty and to be very jungly indeed. The Palace was
most ornate with coloured glass everywhere, very ornate furniture,
etc. We had quite good illuminations after dinner, which we saw
from the roof. HE was taken to the station by the Maharajah in a
car which was made the shape of a swan with scarlet inside!!

We first stopped yesterday for lunch with the Maharajah of Jindi,
and had to sit through a ten course lunch which took us over an
hour to get through. My neighbour was a young Indian in a frock-
coat. I think he was the private secretary – he never missed one
single thing on the menu and he did not burst. The Jind army
consists of 400 men only, but there are two Generals here, one a
full blown Major-General in a scarlet tunic, frightfully tight, and
the other was a Brigade General, also in a scarlet tunic. Jindi
himself is practically stone deaf so HE had a cheery meal!!

Then we arrived at Maler Kotla for tea; a huge tea in a very
charming Palace, very well built and very nicely decorated. HE
had promised to stop for two minutes to say a few words at Bagrian,
between Maler Kotla and Nabbha, to an old man there who had

done well in recruiting. When we got there, we found the main
Road blocked by police and a large crowd, and the side road to this
old man's house all beflagged and lined with people, etc., so there
was nothing for it but for HE to go there; a salute was fired and
the old man had prepared a programme to last for half an hour.
However, HE did not get out of his car even, as it was a real big
bounce on his part. He succeeded in delaying us for quite ten
minutes or more, which was rather a bore as we were fifteen
minutes late leaving Maler Kotla thanks to that chap Renouf who
asked after you and your stamps, but whom I did not think much of
all the same. Crump is getting these stamps for you from Jind and
Nabbha, but Maler Kotla has not got any stamps at all.

Much love

Ralph

November 3rd, 1919                    Viceregal Lodge, Delhi

My own Darling,

I have not yet heard from you from Dehra, but I hope all is well.
HE opened the chiefs' conference today with a long and most
excellent speech. The chiefs' conference is to be an officially
constituted body now recognised by the Secretary of State; those
chiefs who are entitled to attend are to be called ruling Princes,
and the others are to be known as ruling Chiefs . . .

November 5th, 1919                    Viceregal Lodge, Delhi

. . .

Her Ex. did an awfully stupid thing in Dehra Dun – she insisted
on going into a Hindu temple which was really closed to Europeans.
Mrs Crosthwaite was with her at the time, and was in a most awful
funk that they would be attacked or at any rate insulted; she
apparently wrote to Her Ex. afterwards, and protested about it, but
got no answer. She then wrote very strongly to Cuffs about it, who
gave me the letter and asked me to take action about it. It is such a
very stupid thing to have done and Mrs Crosthwaite described in

great detail the insulting remarks which were made about them by the Hindus there, and in fact the threatening gestures, etc.*

I sent this letter straight into the Viceroy with a note saying that Her Ex. probably did not realise her danger in doing a thing like that, but that after what happened in Burma at those temples I felt bound to bring it to their notice, and begged that she would not do such a thing again. He sent a letter back to me thanking me for sending him Mrs Crosthwaite's letter and writing 'I have talked to Her Excellency'!! This apparently happened while I was at Mohand, and I think Mrs Crosthwaite was much frightened that it would get into the press. She insisted on going in because she thought she might like to sketch it! What an awful fool Her Ex. really is!!! . . .

*Mrs Crosthwaite: the wife of Lt-Colonel Charles Crosthwaite (1878–1940) who served in the Third Afghan War.

Monday, midday, November 9th, 1919        Lalloarh, Bikanir, Rajputana

My own Darling,

I am waiting here for my train to Delhi which only leaves at 2.30 p.m.

The Maharajah very kindly gave me one of his saloons to come back in as far as this place which is the terminus of his line, so I spent a luxurious night, and can have my meals in it as he sent a cook and food.

Very much love, your own

Ralph

*Nita to Ralph's mother*

November 13th, 1919        Dun Court, Dehra Dun

My dear Mother,

David nearly had a nasty accident the other day; he was bolted with while sitting in his basket on the back of our old grey donkey,

Ebenezer. It is Joscelyne's donkey, and he rides it occasionally in this basket; we never thought the donkey had so much as a kick in him, but Kim, our terrier, bolted out of the house, frightened him and off he went. He knocked Nurse over and careered away, with the unfortunate David bobbing about. The basket started to slide and went over further and further; all the servants joined in the chase, poor Nurse who had picked herself up quite stunned, gave chase too. The basket got lower and lower, David was hanging head down held in by a strap, screaming of course and adding to the donkey's terror. Kim, too, had kept up all the time yapping with joy, naturally. One of our sentries managed to catch up; he could not stop the donkey, but hauled David out who was literally upside down between the donkey's legs. The donkey still went on, and was caught over a mile away from the house, in a deep ravine.

You can imagine poor Nurse's feelings, she was badly bruised and grazed, her hair down to her knees, but the precious David safe in her arms. I was out with the others, picnicking. The most agonising part of it all was when the sentry, armed with a bayonet, instead of dropping it ran with it stretched straight before him at the donkey. Nurse's one thought was if the donkey turned sharply, it would go into David. I am glad I was not there. Nurse was so shaken she could hardly move next day; David, of course, was as happy as he could be, two minutes later.

Our Guard are a great source of amusement; there are six on duty at the gates, and whenever I go out whether in the motor or pushing David's pram or leading the donkey, they all tumble out, stand to attention and salute. John takes the salute for me quite seriously!

John still delights in Knights and battles, and told me the other day that he really thought he would turn into a second Don Quixote who is one of his favourite characters in the many books that I read him.

Your very affectionate

Nita

*Ralph to Nita's father*

November 20th, 1919                    Viceregal Lodge, Delhi

My dear Daddy,

I am here for one day only, starting off again on tour tomorrow to Madras and South India; I got back this morning from Lucknow, where the Viceroy spent three days on an official visit. I had not been there since 1907, when I went over from Shahjehanpur, in January, as a subaltern from the 2nd Rifle Brigade, for a race meeting and a big Ball. A Mr Hilton, a mutiny veteran, showed us all over the Old Residency at Lucknow the other day, which he helped to defend against the mutineers in July and August 1857, as a young lad of about sixteen or seventeen; he showed us where he stood, the remains of the room where his father and mother lived, and it was thrilling to listen to the account of the siege from the fine old soldier.

We had a most picturesque march past the Viceroy of all the schools in Lucknow, in different coloured turbans, preceded by elephants in their processional gold trappings, and that evening the Talugdars of Oudh, who are wealthy landed proprietors only less important than Maharajahs, gave a reception in a colossal shamiana, followed by a torchlight tattoo by the Norfolk regiment and fireworks, all the buildings along the road being illuminated.

Now we go off to a very different climate and very different scenery, with a long journey of three nights to Madras; the most interesting thing we shall see will probably be a Keddah, or wild elephant hunt, driving them into different enclosures of log fences. This is in Mysore and only comes off about once in every five or seven years; I am told that a good Keddah means the capture of about seventy wild elephants, who will be put through the first process of being tamed by being tied up to the strong fencing, bordering the enclosures.

Calcutta from Dec. 14th to Jan. 11th will be a busy time, with an official visit to Benares on the way back to Delhi, followed by a conference here from Jan. 18th to 25th of all Governors and Lt. Governors in India; my fourth year as Military Secretary will thus be coming to an end!

Yours very affectionately

Ralph

35. Celebrations: Shan tribesmen dressed as animals, Mandalay

36. K.S. Barne's allegorical play in Viceregal Lodge Gardens, 1917

37. Recreation: a party returning by motor boat

38. A shooting party stuck in flood

39. On a riding holiday, left to right: Nita, Miss Owen, W. Holland-Hibbert

40. Nita on left; W. Holland-Hibbert, right

41.  Part of the Maharajah's Palace at Gwalior

42.  The Viceroy at the Proclamation Parade, January 1st 1918, Bombay

*Ralph to Nita*

November 24th, 1919                    Government House, Madras

My own Darling,

A great arrival here this morning with a good procession up from the station. Lady Willingdon has absolutely transformed this house altogether and has made it most awfully nice. She is a wonderful woman; after breakfast she was all over the place visiting every single member of the party in their rooms to see that things were all right, even the Maids she inspected. We went into Cuffs' bedroom but he was not to be seen though there were ominous rustlings from the bathroom, however Lady W. was not the least put out, talked loudly, so he might know she was there, about his room and how airy it was, etc., and then passed on to the next room.

I wish you could see our programme for this visit. I found on my table a mass of literature quite a foot high, but to my relief I found there were fourteen copies in this pile of our full programme, with long accounts of each institute or hospital Their Ex's are to visit, lists of the motors told off to the various members of the party, lists of dates for the ADCs, plans of the house, maps of Madras, etc. etc. etc. Really the printing press here must have been kept busy. They seem to have a large staff; Goldie as Military Secretary does not do more than is absolutely necessary I should say; that little chap de Brath is here as extra ADC, rather a little bounder, isn't he? It is pretty hot and one must stay close to the fan.

HE is receiving addresses the whole of this morning; there is a lunch party at 1.30 p.m. then an official visit and return visit with the Maharajah of Travancore after lunch, a chance of a game of golf at Adyar in the evening, and a large dinner party tonight. We start things at 8 a.m. tomorrow morning, and end up with an investiture and perhaps an informal dance in the evening afterwards, for those who care to stay for it; what a life!!*

Very much love my own darling,

Ralph

---

*Major Kenneth Oswald Goldie (1882–1938) was Military Secretary to the Governor of Madras 1919–24. He had previously been ADC to Lord Minto.

*This Letter Came By Aeroplane From India In 1919*
*Nita to her sister in Australia*

November 25th, 1919                    Viceregal Lodge, Delhi

Darling Sissiekins,

Ross Smith takes this out, so I can give you all the latest news of the family. Since I got back from Dehra I have had a series of adventures; people here laugh over my capability of having them, it's really a disease! I hadn't been back two days before I was tossed by a cow, which bruised me very much, then had a midnight adventure with an Indian I found in my drawing-room, and finally, funniest of all, pursued a runaway cart with Lady Hudson, the wife of the Adjutant-General, a very severe governess type of woman with pince-nez perched on the extreme tip of her sharp nose. I dragged her out of the shop and made her come to the rescue with me, much to the amusement of the passers-by. We caught it and led it back along the wall, only to find that it was a most odiferous sewage cart![1]

The babies are very happy at Dehra, and I am more than busy with my shop. It is a great concern this year. I just love it and slave there from 7 a.m. to 7 p.m. It's most fascinating, especially the books and toys.[2]

Best love to you all from

Mid

[1]Sir Ross Smith (1892–1922) and his brother Keith completed the first flight from Britain to Australia between 12 November and 10 December, 1919, in a Vickers Vimy bomber powered by two Rolls Royce Eagle engines. Sir Ross was killed in a flying accident near Brooklands aerodrome, England on April 13th, 1922.
[2]A charity shop in aid of the Red Cross Society in India.

*Ralph to Nita*

November 26th, 1919                    Viceroy's Camp, Madras

My own Darling,

Everything here has gone off well, but we have had a really strenuous programme to carry out. Yesterday HE was on the go from 8 a.m. till 11.15 p.m. The reception last night was very crowded, and both Their Ex's shook hands with something like just under 1,000 guests.

I have just written letters for presents for all the staff, etc., and have got everything ready for our departure tonight. We dine at the Adyar club and go straight from there to the station. I went out sightseeing with the Viceroy this morning, and among other things we went to the Government House at Guindy about six miles from here, a most delightful place in a large park; the Willingdons want to live out there altogether, and turn this Government House into the secretariat.

We had a very tiring ceremony of the laying of a foundation stone this morning at 8.30 a.m. in full dress and in the blazing sun. The sheriff of Madras, an Indian, made an interminably long speech. I do not think Her Ex. could live at this place for long, in this climate!!

Your own

Ralph


December 1st, 1919                    Viceroy's Camp, Mysore

. . .

We got here this morning and it was one of the best shows I have seen, all the crowds in this part of India turn out in thousands and cheer and clap like anything which makes such a difference, all their clothing is so picturesque. The Viceroy's return visit to the Maharajah was a wonderful sight, though there were very few sirdars etc. in the Hall. But a lot of attendants preceded HE and the Maharajah, with a sort of sweeping and salaaming and singing and weird sort of cry. The Durbar room was very garish but it all fitted in, and a string band played oriental music most awfully well during the visit.

Very much love, your

Ralph

December 4th, 1919                          Viceroy's Camp, Mysore

My own Darling.

We had a very good show last night here at the Palace, which was quite dark till HE passed through the gates, then suddenly the whole Palace was illuminated like a flash of lightning, by simply turning on one switch, with 35,000 electric lights. We went upstairs onto a covered-in balcony with pillars, overlooking the courtyard where about 200 or more men were paraded in white uniforms in open order; suddenly all the lights went out and equally suddenly the torches which each man carried, one in each hand, all blazed up, the band started and they did club swinging to music with these flaming torches – it was most effective. At the end of the performance they marched to the back of the courtyard, and as they went out lit up something which was lying on the ground; when this something was raised up (it was a kind of frame work standing at least twenty feet high) it turned out to be the word 'Chelmsford' and a blaze of welcome appeared at the top of the courtyard above it.

After this we went to the Durbar Hall, in the centre of which were sitting the Indian Band which was quite good, then went into the organ room where he has got an electric organ played like the pianola; the whole of the end of the room is a mass of organ pipes. The Maharajah is very musical himself, he plays the violin and the piano; altogether it was a short but amusing evening.

Yesterday afternoon we went out by motor to Seringapatam which is only nine miles or so from here, and we saw all over it; most interesting; we saw the spot where Tippo was wounded, the place where his body was eventually found in the middle of a whole pile of dead bodies. We saw the dungeons where our wretched prisoners in his hands were kept chained up to the wall. A Col. Bayley was imprisoned here for nearly eighteen months and then died. We had tea in Tippo's summer palace; it is a huge palace on an island, not his palace but the whole of Seringapatam Fort, with large ramparts; it must have been a most difficult place to take in those days; we saw the spot where the breech was made in the walls, and where our men rushed across the river and stopped the breech. The date was 1799, at the end of May, so the heat must have been terrific.*

Your own

Ralph

*Tippo Sahib (1751–99) son of Haider Ali, was Sultan of Mysore 1782–99. He was killed in action at the storming of Seringapatam in the Fourth Mysore War.

December 5th, 1919                                    Keddah Camp

My own Darling,

We got here yesterday afternoon, and in the evening went on to the actual Keddah which is about five miles from here. We all stood behind a screen made of bamboos, above the river. After a long wait we saw the elephants coming up the river, being driven along by the trained elephants behind them; they had come out of the jungle some way below us. Whenever they tried to get to one bank or the other, the crowds of coolies made a great noise and lit fires on the bank in order to keep them in the river. A herd of about twenty-four passed us, they were really very tame and were prodded and pushed along.

They could only get up the river bank at the place which led into the stockade; when they were in that a big gate was shut down, so that they could not get out. A big ditch enclosing about five acres is dug; elephants cannot jump so really when they were in this enclosure they could not get out, even if there had been no stockade. The ditch must be about ten feet deep and perhaps fifteen feet wide, with bamboo sticks across it and bamboo hurdles banking up the sides to prevent the elephants falling in.

This morning operations started at 8 a.m. and they were trying, the whole morning, to drive this herd from the large five-acre enclosure through a narrow passage into a smaller enclosure.

They got them right up into the opening time and time again, but they always broke back through the line of the beating elephants. They gave it up at 12 o'clock and started again at 3 p.m. when they succeeded almost straight away. All the larger elephants were driven into the smaller enclosure and the gate was then shut down. Five quite small ones were caught in the narrow passage between the two; large trained elephants then came into this passage, after the small ones had been fastened to the stockade by ropes.

Two large elephants got the smaller ones in between them, and then ropes were got round the necks of the small ones and fastened right round the tummies of the big ones. This took a long time. Part of the stockade passage was then removed and the little wild elephants were led away down the road like prisoners, each one between the two trained elephants.

They had to rope one big cow elephant in the large stockade which they managed to do somehow; she was very wild so they had four trained elephants for her, two in front and two behind, to all four of which she was fastened by ropes so she could not do much. It certainly is a very interesting thing to see, but I confess the wild elephants do not fight as I thought they would; in fact, all this morning reminded me of a sheepdog trial trying to drive a lot of sheep through a pen!

Tomorrow we are going to see the large elephants who are in the small enclosure, roped. On Sunday I hope to go out bison shooting with HE, the rest of the party are going after tiger.

We go out on two elephants, and I believe we can get quite close up to them.

Very much love,
Your own

Ralph

December 6th, 1919                                   Keddah Camp

My own Darling,

We have been out again to the Keddah this morning, and it was most thrilling. Last night we left the bulk of the herd in the small stockade, and the job this morning was the roping of them and taking them off into the jungle to tie them up to trees, and so gradually tame them. Operations started at 10 a.m. HE went out fishing at 7 a.m. and he was to come back to see the Keddah by

10 a.m. but instead of doing so, he sent back word to say he was busy catching a big fish and could not come till later, so we started without him.

First the big gate was opened to let in about eighteen trained elephants which, with about fifteen wild elephants in already, made a tremendous squash in this small stockade; elephants wild and tame were jostling each other all over the place, and the danger seemed to me to be lest one of the mahouts should fall off his elephant and be trampled to death.

The mahouts were very clever and by backing their elephants and manoeuvring them, they got one of the wild ones isolated from the rest, and they formed a wall between him and the rest of the herd. Then men came in on foot, and by going behind this wild elephant which was jammed between several other tame ones, they got ropes round his hind legs which they fastened to the stockade. Then the tame elephants pushed him towards it by degrees, while the men in the stockade drew in the rope until at last he was held fast, by the back legs securely tied up to the stockade. This process was repeated to most of the others, until about eight wild elephants were all fastened to the stockade by ropes tied round their hind legs. Then the mahouts proceeded to lassoo them round the neck with large looped ropes; this was rather difficult, but by jamming them tight between the tame elephants and slipping the big loops right over their heads, they managed to do this all right and the ends were fastened also to the stockade.

Some of the smaller ones were only lassooed by the neck, and not tied by the leg at all. But the biggest one, which was a tusker, had naturally to be fastened to no less than five trained elephants before he was taken out of the stockade. When all the wild elephants had been secured, and this took quite two hours to do, the gate was hauled up and the biggest wild one, fastened to his five keepers, was hauled and pushed out of the stockade down a narrow passage to the river. He was followed by all the other ones; some of the quite tiny baby elephants being just pulled along by the large tame elephants, with a rope round its neck. They all splashed into the river, were taken down about a quarter of a mile and then were led up into the jungle, where they were tied up to trees.

HE has caught a lot of fish, the biggest one being forty-four lbs so he is quite happy, but I do not really call it much sport, as he stands on the bank and has a line thrown in with a large lump of atta on the end of it, very much like we did in Patiala in that tank fishing; however he seems to enjoy it.

Your own

Ralph


December 8th, 1919                              Keddah Camp

My own Darling,

Maffey tells me that orders have been issued, or are going to be issued, for everybody next year to live out in New Delhi except HE and his household and members of council; all the military people and secretaries to Government and all other officials are to live out there – this will make a tremendous change; how people will hate it.

News on the frontier are going very well. The Mahsuds are coming in today and tomorrow, we have now really only to deal with the Wazirs near Wana. I think our aeroplanes have done very well, and have shown that we possess a weapon of offense against these tribes which may be very valuable in the future.

Your own

Ralph


December 17th, 1919                    Viceroy's Camp, Calcutta

My own Darling,

No letter yet from you this morning. I dined at Government House last night, and was taken up to Lady Ronaldshay who asked after you and said 'I like your wife so much and I love her clothes; she is the best dressed woman in India', so that ought to please you! She talked about the children, and that day she went up into the nursery and saw them in pyjamas going to bed.[1]

How very like Ross Smith to divide up the £10,000 equally among his party, which I hear he has done, saying that they all took equal risks; it was a splendid performance and I think he deserves a knighthood just as much as those two who crossed the Atlantic.[2]

I have also got rather bad news from the North West Frontier in Waziristan; there is no doubt that General Skeen has had a knock; there are thirteen British officers killed or missing, and our casualties are about 200, although a later wire says that our objectives were all gained in subsequent operations. I kept this news from HE until we came back from church and did not mean to let him see it until after lunch, but Maffey and I were talking it over when he walked into the office. It is rather worrying as it will probably delay the final subjection of these tribes. We seem to have allowed the Mahsuds to get round us, and two regiments, namely the 55th Coke's rifles and the 103rd, bolted, or that is what it looks like at present. Do not say anything about this of course; another brigade has been sent up in support of General Skeen.

So what with these telegrams, and the arrangements in connection with Her Ex's operation, I have had rather a disturbed Sunday morning.[3]

*Later:*

Cuffs tells me that the operation was quite successful, but that it was most necessary to have had it done. He says that they will not know for perhaps ten days the result of the two pathological examinations they are making of what came out, but Cuffs thinks that the trouble is not really over and that Her Ex. will have more haemorrhages again. However, he says he cannot say more than that until the result of the examinations is known, but had she not had this operation she could not possibly have got better.

Very much love,
Your own

Ralph

[1]Wife of the Earl of Ronaldshay, later 2nd Marquess of Zetland (1876–1961). He was Governor of Bengal 1917–22 and Secretary of State for India, 1935–40.
[2]Ross Smith was given a knighthood and a prize of £10,000 by the Australian Government for his flight from England to Australia.
[3]Lady Chelmsford was suffering from irregular haemorrhages.

# CHAPTER TEN

The Viceroy stays in Calcutta until 10th January, 1920. Problems between the Viceroy and Montagu about the Amritsar show in the Punjab. A further investiture, another State Ball and another parade. By January 24th the Viceroy is back in Delhi for another Governors' Conference, and on the 25th Ralph goes to Madras to meet the Duke of Connaught. Joan is married in style in Delhi. The Viceroy pays a visit to Gwalior. Ralph accompanies Nita and family to Bombay for their visit to Australia and returns to Gwalior and then back to Simla.

At the end of April the Prince of Rumania pays a visit. Problems over General Dyer's conduct in the Punjab, problems over the Military Secretary's staff's salaries and regimental soldiers' pay. Excitement in Australia over the Prince of Wales' visit there, and problems over his postponing his visit to India.

*Ralph to Nita*

December 24th, 1919                      Viceroy's Camp, Calcutta

My own Darling,

I did think Montagu's references to the information he received about the Amritsar show in the Punjab riots perfectly monstrous. I think he is reported to have said that the first he knew about it was the announcement in the papers. I am afraid there is no doubt that he is trying to clear himself of any responsibility or blame, and to make it appear that the Viceroy kept back all news about it. It is so different to Chamberlain's attitude over the Mespot. business; he insisted on sharing the responsibility for it and so resigned, which may have been quixotic but one could not help admiring him for it. Montagu, on the other hand, is obviously trying to down HE over it and also O'Dwyer. Do not say anything about it, but things at present are rather acute and a pretty sharp telegram went home yesterday from HE to the Secretary of State, giving him the number and the dates of the telegrams which were sent from here at that time, so that he can look them up for himself – which he certainly will not do.*

The *Times* saying there were 2,000 casualties is a gross exaggeration too, of course. However, I think we must wait for the result of the Hunter commission report; they are writing it now in Bombay. I must say I think Maffey is awfully good in these sorts of things – he says the great thing is for HE to keep his temper and not send any telegram which Montagu could take hold of as an ultimatum, and say that either you or I must go sort of thing.

Very much love and a happy Xmas,
Your own

Ralph

*Ralph is referring to the Amritsar affair (13 April, 1919) when General Dyer (1864–1927) marched a detachment of soldiers to a square crowded with Indians assembled in defiance of his orders and opened fire on them, killing 400 and wounding many more. Dyer was forced to resign in March, 1920.

December 25th, 1919                    Viceroy's Camp, Calcutta

My own Darling,

You will have seen that it is now announced about the coming of the Prince of Wales. I expect Mrs Maffey will be very sick that he has resigned now!!!

We have got our Xmas dinner tonight with a dance afterwards, about 300 altogether including both functions; we shall probably have about 1,000 for Jan. 1st. I am dining with the Vaux's tonight, before the dance here at Government House. The Ronaldshay children are dining here tonight.*

Apparently, between ourselves, the Amir is now making overtures for a permanent peace with us. HE is inclined is say that he has not given any sign of being generally friendly to us yet, which was laid down in the first treaty as a condition on which we would consider new relations with him, but Maffey is trying to persuade HE that these overtures are a sign of that, and that these overtures should not be repulsed. I suppose this will be discussed in Council which meets here on the 31st. I do not know enough of what has passed to be able to form an opinion yet, but of course it means a good deal to Maffey if the first treaty is ratified by this second one, as the whole suggestion originated with him.

Very much love my own darling,
Your own

Ralph

*Lt-Col. Henry Vaux (1883–1957) was Military Secretary to the Earl of Ronaldshay 1917–22. He had been Military Secretary to Lord Carmichael from 1914 to 1917. His wife was an American called Baroness Edna von Stockhausen.

December 26th, 1919                    Viceroy's Camp, Calcutta

My own Darling,

It is simply splendid about 12 Connaught Place having been sold. I am most awfully relieved about it and I think my mother was lucky to get £2,000 for it. I am really most awfully glad about it.

Our procession on to the race course was a great success, and the Body Guard made a very good show. Margaret went in the first carriage with HE and Joan, and stayed for three races. Anne, Miss Ridley, Maffey and I went in the second carriage; we had all the stewards up on turn in the box, and the wives came to tea with HE. I made about fifty Rs. this afternoon. Yes, Maffey did very well the other day, but then he bets pretty heavily. He put 500 Rs. each way on that horse, that is 1,000 Rs. altogether, which I call pretty heavy betting. I confine myself to the tote getting a ten Rs. ticket.

In April 1919, an English missionary doctor in Amritsar was attacked and left for dead; in retaliation, Brig. General Dyer killed some 400 Indians in Amritsar, and the Lt. Governor of the Punjab, Sir Michael O'Dwyer, was held responsible.

Montagu has been perfectly damnable the last few days. He sends this sort of telegram: 'Public Opinion at home intensely inflamed, I really cannot allow this to continue, much feeling over action of General O'Dwyer, I really cannot understand why you did not relieve O'Dwyer of his duties when Lt. Governor and have a court of enquiry on his conduct.' And then he has the impudence to end up with 'Merry Xmas'!!! I repeat that I think Maffey's attitude is excellent, he keeps very calm and is very clever at putting the matter before HE in as conciliatory a light as possible. The great thing is not to let HE send any telegram which can give Montagu the opportunity of using it as an ultimatum. Maffey and I usually talk things over in the motor going to golf or something, and he is very good in allowing me to tell him exactly what I should do.

Of course, O'Dwyer knows absolutely nothing about these kinds of telegram, but I went out with him yesterday morning in a car and O'Dwyer gave me his unvarnished opinion of Montagu. Yesterday HE was very worried about the whole thing. The monstrous thing is that Montagu sends out the Hunter Commission to investigate the whole question, and then prejudges it before their report has been written.

You may, however, have noticed that when Montagu announced, in the House in answer to a question, that O'Dwyer had not been superseded or relieved of his duties, there were loud cheers in the House; this does not quite support his statement that public opinion intensely inflamed over O'Dwyer's action and that the Viceroy ought to have practically put O'Dwyer under arrest!! However, things will come all right if HE will only keep his temper, and I frankly confess Maffey is doing jolly well, in my humble opinion.

The Mahsuds have given in, and have accepted our peace terms although they are now very much harsher than they were at first; this is a great relief. The Amir is also again trying to enter into permanent peace negotiations with us. Tony Grant is, of course, all for it and so is Maffey. I was trying to persuade the latter yesterday not to show his hand too clearly, and not to give the Amir the impression that we were in any hurry to fix up a permanent peace with him yet, but of course both he and Grant feel that if this could come off now, it would prove their policy of six months ago to have been sound.

Your own

Ralph

December 30th, 1919                          Viceroy's Camp, Calcutta

My own Darling,

The Verney hostel seems to be doing excellent work and to be immensely appreciated by a good many people. I am sure you have made a good many real friends who have every cause to be grateful to you.

You will have seen that Mrs John and Mrs Parsons have got the MBE; why Mrs Maffey was given the OBE and Mrs John and Nellie the MBE is difficult to explain. HE is awfully sick about Lord Montagu of Beaulieu having been given the KCIE. HE strongly opposed it on the ground that his work for India had not been such as to deserve such a high decoration; he pointed this out most carefully to the Secretary of State, in one of his letters. Lord Montagu actually wrote out a description of his own services in India, in a memorandum to the Secretary of State, which I saw and read some time ago. It was in the form of a final report on the mechanical Transport and roads on the frontier in India, but in point of fact it was nothing more nor less than an account of the services which Lord M. considered he had rendered to India. How any man can have the cheek to do a thing like that I cannot conceive, however the result is a KCIE!! It really is rather monstrous, especially when one thinks of the enjoyable trips all round the world he took at the public expense, and the very little amount of work he did out here.

Your own

Ralph


January 2nd, 1920                                    Viceroy's Camp, India
                                                                    Calcutta

My own Darling,

Our show last night was a great success, and I have never seen HE so pleased with any function before. His only criticism was that as it was so good, it was rather a pity we did not make it a full dress show. Maffey was not nearly as good as little Holland; in the investiture part of it he did not shout out the names nearly loud enough, nor did he do it as impressively as Holland. However that is only my opinion. The Body Guard looked very well, and John had done wonders with the supper room decorations. We kept up the dancing till about 1.30 a.m. I danced a lot with Lady Monro. I also danced with Lady Ronaldshay and Lady Wheeler, but I did not make up the programme because I really wanted to be free to go about looking after things, and there were a good many people to look after in the way of the C-in-C, the Ronaldshays, Maharajahs, etc. Old Kashmir was there, and I had to lead the old man by the hand the whole way up the Ball Room to see HE but I was able to push him off quite early.*

I have just got the news from Her Ex. that she has lost the Crown of India Order!! She does not know where she dropped it, or what she has done with it!!! Of course the whole house has to be searched for the beastly thing now. She cannot remember whether she took it off her dress when she went to bed – the only thing she knows is that she cannot find it now! She has got to wear it tonight for a dinner at Government House, so you can imagine what a fuss she is in!!!

*Later:*

The CIO was found on the floor in the supper room, so all is well again; perhaps next time she will see that it is pinned onto her dress securely. Our numbers last night were 1,020; that was not too many for the size of the room and the dancing was not at all too crowded; of course after supper a lot of people cleared off.

Your own

Ralph

*Lady Wheeler was the wife of Sir Henry Wheeler (1870–1950), then Member of the Executive Council, Bengal (1917–22). He had been Home Secretary, Government of the India 1912–16. He later became Governor of Bihar and Orissa, 1922–27.

January 8th, 1920                    Viceroy's Camp, Calcutta

My own Darling,

Her Ex. at this moment is going round the house with Coryton and John, making the most absurd proposals about pulling the whole place to pieces. She says the girls want the ADCs' room as their sitting-room, my office is to be cut in half, and apparently the ADCs and I are to share it!! I am simply letting her blow off steam, but I have not the slightest intention of sanctioning her suggestions. I suppose at the outside she will be in Belvedere another three weeks while she is in India. Except for a few quite small alterations, the present arrangements have served admirably and I think it much better to let them stand for our last visit; besides which, I know HE will certainly not allow an immense amount of money to be spent on this place again, so as it would have been a pure waste of my time going round the whole place with her, I am sitting here in my room and shall have a talk to Coryton afterwards.*

We shall have to spend a lot of money this next year over the Prince of Wales' visit, and there is no reason in the world why Her Ex. should spend a huge amount on this place, especially as I do not think it will be possible for the Viceroy to be in Calcutta at the same time as the P. of W. Lord Ronaldshay has been so awfully good about the whole question of the Viceroy coming to Calcutta that I am sure he will be allowed to run his own show for the Prince of Wales, and that the Viceroy will be most anxious not to queer his pitch by coming here himself just at that time, at least that is only my own impression. I never mention the P. of W. to the Viceroy, and I really know nothing about his visit yet.

*Air Chief Marshal Sir William Alec Coryton served with the Rifle Brigade in the First World War; transferred to RAF 1917; Flying Instructor to HM King George VI when Duke of York, 1919; served on N.W.F. India, 1920.

*Ralph to his mother*

January 24th, 1920                                    Viceregal Lodge, Delhi

My dearest Mother,

I have sent you home this week the certificate in connection with the Order of the Sacred Treasure of Japan. It is interesting chiefly because the signature at the top is the actual signature of the Emperor. The Japanese military attaché came by appointment to my office and presented it to me. Apparently the Emperor signs these with his own hand for the 1st, 2nd and 3rd classes of this order. I think it is quite interesting enough to keep, so I send it home to you.

We have just had the annual week of the Governors' Conference and every corner here has been full up; this next week we have the Admiral, his wife and staff coming, as well as the Maharajah of Kapurthala and a good many other people as well, for a small dance here on Monday and another private dance at the club on Wednesday. We had four dinner parties here this last week, so we are actually having a quiet time.

I have had to arrange a ceremony for installing the Flag and Shield presented by Queen Alexandra on behalf of the Women of England, to the Indian Army. This takes place on Friday morning next, on the occasion of the opening of the legislative Council.

Very much love

Ralph

*Ralph to his mother*

March 19th, 1920　　　　　　　　　　　　Viceregal Lodge, Delhi

My dearest Mother,

Nita is due to leave here [for Australia] on the 23rd, Tuesday morning next, and will stay for the night of the 24th in Bombay at Admiralty House, sailing on the 25th in the *Chemintz*.

I have had a very busy week indeed. On Tuesday was Joan's wedding, and I really think it went off splendidly. I took Joan and HE to church by motor, all the others having gone on ahead; after the service which only lasted twenty minutes, the bride and bridegroom left the church in a State Carriage drawn by four grey horses, with postillions in scarlet livery, Their Ex.s following in the second State Carriage with myself, an ADC and the Body Guard, big scarlet and gold umbrellas being held over their heads by servants standing up behind. This procession came back to Viceregal Lodge, and on our return the wedding photographs were taken, then we went down into the garden where all the guests were assembled, and they all passed through a shamiana in which Joan and her husband stood receiving congratulations and good wishes.

The huge wedding cake was about six feet high and was made by one of our Indian cooks. Joan cut it with Lascelles' sword and the C-in-C proposed their healths. I had the drums and pipers of the Seaforth Highlanders over from Meerut which kept things going fairly during the reception, and played alternatively with the Viceroy's band. The motor was ready for them at 6 p.m. and about 6.10 p.m. they left for Meerut where they stayed the night and then went on to Dehra Dun the next day, and are going to Kashmir on the 28th. I think everything worked out exactly to my time-table.

Hignell, our new private secretary, arrived today. I like him immensely. Maffey leaves on Wednesday, and sails on Saturday for home. He is probably coming out again next winter as one of the political officers attending to the Prince of Wales. I sincerely hope his wife does not come too!!

Your very affectionate

Ralph

*Ralph to Nita*

May 5th, 1920                                   Viceregal Lodge, Simla

My own Darling,

I have really had a very busy weekend with the Roumanian Invasion. I took charge of them for the whole of Saturday and Sunday; we had a lunch party at Annandale followed by the usual futile gymkhana. HRH dined with the Chief that night so I had the staff to Curzon House to dine, and took them to the theatre afterwards. On Sunday, I took them to the Retreat for the day, and I dined up there with them that evening, with two of our ADCs. On Monday we had our first dance, which was a great success. HRH did not dance at all, so he was kept supplied with people to talk to all the evening. The party finally left yesterday evening, and when I arrived at Sumner Hill Station all his staff came up and congratulated me warmly on the high decoration which HRH had bestowed on me.

I knew nothing of this, but HE this morning presented me with the 'Order of the Crown of Roumania with swords'. I believe that is what it is called, but I have written to find out. I do not know whether I shall be allowed to wear it or not, but it is rather a jolly ornamented decoration with a red and blue ribbon. HE was given the first class of the same order. HRH also gave me, through HE, five decorations of a lower order for the ADCs, but I am keeping them all, including my own, till we get orders from home about them. Anyway, I shall give one to John Mackenzie and leave out one of the ADCs. Medals were also presented to Jordan Anderson and the Sgt. Major, so you see foreign orders and decorations were being fairly showered about!!

By the way, Maffey has got himself appointed the channel of communication between the Government of India and St James's Palace for any questions connected with the Prince's visit, with an office in the India Office. His great need for a rest and holiday seems to have curiously diminished now that the Royal visit is in prospect!! He never said a word about this to me, though apparently he had arranged this before leaving India!!

Your own

Ralph

May 6th, 1920                              Viceregal Lodge, Simla

My own Darling,

Hignell is afraid of telegrams coming from home about the Hunter Commission report. We certainly had a very nasty one from Montagu this afternoon, which I had to deal with as it came through the Army Department.

It was about General Dyer. General D. came up to Simla before going home, and the doctors said he was so mentally ill that any prolonged worry might prove fatal. The Chief had him up and told him frankly that he must resign his command, and that he must not expect to be re-employed again in India. The action taken by the Chief was reported to Montagu by letter which went on April 12th and which, therefore, must be with Montagu by now, but because this was not sent by wire, he sends a furious telegram asking why he was not informed at once of the action taken by the Chief and saying that we have made it impossible for the Cabinet to take any disciplinary action against Dyer, etc. etc.

Of course, it is an easy and popular thing to say that Dyer saved the Punjab, but still the Viceroy and the whole of his Council including the C-in-C decided that he was to blame to a certain extent, after a most careful and prolonged consideration, so it isn't proper for anybody less well informed to say that they were wrong in their judgement. One must feel sorry for Dyer, everybody does, but sympathy should not be allowed to influence a judicial and impartial judgement on the facts of the case. It still remains to be seen what is the published opinion of the Hunter Commission, but that ought to be out this week.

Scindia has sent me a most charming cigarette case, a gold one with the following inscription: 'From M.S. to R.V. as an affectionate memento of the week spent together from 15th to 20th April 1920 in the jungles of Sheppur. Gwalior.' After giving me the jolliest six days' holiday I have ever had, he goes and sends me a gold cigarette case as a memento!!

I am going to fight a case with the Army Pay department. My pay this month came to 909 Rs!! They have charged me rent for our bungalow in Delhi and for Curzon House since July 1st, 1919 and they propose to go on charging me. It really is monstrous, and of course I shall not stand it for a moment. I shall get the Viceroy to pass orders about it, if necessary; nobody else on the staff has been asked to pay this because I am the only one who is paid from military funds, all the others are paid from Civil. After four years' work here, I have no intention of having my pay reduced to 909 Rs. a month for the next four months or so, in order to make up back payments of what they are pleased to call rent, which is what the DDO Lucknow informs me that he intends to do. We shall see!!!!!!

My best love to the children,
Your own husband

Ralph

May 27th, 1920                                    Viceregal Lodge, Simla

My own Darling

We had the most awful night for our Drawing-room on Tuesday. It started to rain about 5 p.m. and it simply poured as hard as it could till midnight. However, in spite of that, the Drawing-room was really a very great success and HE was awfully pleased with the show. John M. also said he had never known any Drawing-room go off so smoothly and so quickly. Old Hignell rang me up on Wednesday morning and felt bound to congratulate me on the success of it; we had eight officers from Army HQ whom I told off for various duties, also Harvey and Poynder from Armsdell.

The Ballroom looked very well indeed, with a large Throne Canopy and two banners of the Star of India and the Indian Empire which I borrowed from the FP Department Body Guard, red and gold carpets, etc. Everybody actually in the Throne room was in full dress, and really the scene was quite a brilliant one. Margaret carried Her Ex.'s train in the procession and looked awfully sweet.

The Thrones were exactly opposite the dining-room; the dais at the end of the room, by the window, was occupied by the Lt.-Governor, the C-in-C and the members of the Council whose wives and daughters joined them after passing their Ex.s. All the ladies came through the big curtains from the big drawing-room, and along the red and gold carpet right across the room opposite the throne. I am afraid it was rather an ordeal for them, especially for the public entrée who had to pass right by all the ladies in the private entrée who, as you can imagine, were watching every curtsey with most critical eyes!!

After the Drawing-room was over, all the private entrée came into supper in the big drawing-room with Their Ex.s, the public entrée having gone straight down to the council chamber. I called out all the names. Anyway I am relieved it is over, especially as it was quite a success.

Our next big show is the State Banquet in full dress on Saturday, 5th June. I think we shall sit down about seventy to dinner, men only; Her Ex. will not be there. I am afraid I shall have trouble with her over the Prince of Wales' visit in Delhi. As there are no ladies, she is not to be included in any procession at all, though of course she will go to everything, but separately by motor, meeting us there; however this was not of course my order, it was settled really by the Viceroy himself, though I do not think she knows it yet!!

The Hunter Commission report [on the massacre at Amritsar] came out last night; I suppose there will be a certain amount of yelling about it, but chiefly directed, I think, against Montagu who will be accused of not having taken drastic action enough against Dyer and O'Dwyer. In fact, the latter is supported in his policy on the whole. I am afraid Dyer gets most of the blame. I will send you the Reuter's report about it.

Your own

Ralph

*Nita to Ralph*

June 7th, 1920                    Arran Kamp, Boural, Australia

My own Darling,

The Prince of Wales was rushed off his feet in Melbourne, thousands and thousands insisted on shaking his hand and following him en masse, he barely got along the streets; no wonder he was dead beat at the end of it and had to postpone his trip here for a week, but I notice that he sticks to Melbourne and is dancing every night, riding or golfing or playing squash, tennis in the afternoons; the latter is his favourite game. Eadith hopes he will use her squash court, as it is the only one in Sydney. He hates big functions and prefers lots of small dances and always wants half a day off to himself, either morning or afternoon or evening. In Melbourne, they never gave him this so the Sydney programme has been very much cut down; you might make a point when arranging his programme in India for the big towns to see that he gets this half day, because he naturally wants to have some time to write letters.*

Your very own

Nita

*Dame Eadith Walker was Nita's cousin

*Ralph to Nita*

June 13th, 1920                                    Viceregal Lodge, Simla

My own Darling,

We had a joke against General Watson the other day. He was riding in uniform and passed HE riding; instead of saluting, Watson took off his cap much to HE's surprise. HE told me about this next morning so I wrote Watson a letter, a copy of which I enclose. He then replied, apologising and suggesting that in future HE in order to be recognised should be asked to always wear his decorations when out riding, and saying he would be only too glad to attend a course of instruction, provided HE would be the instructor and provided the course was held in the covered tennis court, Watson being particularly fond of the game.*

So I then sent him this doggerel, one copy of which I enclose, which seems to have amused him much and which, he wrote back, he will always keep to remind him of an amusing incident. I sent the letter to HE to see, before I sent it to Watson. HE wrote 'excellent' on it, but I did not show him the poem!

Very much love,<br>Your own

Ralph

*Major-General Sir Harry Watson (1866–1945)

?, 1920                                    Viceregal Lodge, Simla

My Dear General,

HE the Viceroy tells me he passed you yesterday evening riding in uniform, and that you raised your cap to him, instead of according to him the usual military salute.

The Viceroy's military experience is, of course, merely that of a Territorial, but he imagines that the raising of the cap when in uniform must be a Regimental custom in the Imperial Service Troops, duly authorised by the military authorities to keep green the memory of some particularly gallant deed in battle, such as the wearing of the regimental badge on the front and back of the cap in the Northamptonshire Regiment.

The only alternative would point to the advisability of a full Major-General being reverted to the 'square' to undergo a refresher course in the art of military saluting!!!

Yours

Ralph Verney


A fine looking General in Uniform clad
Was returning from office one day
His manners were perfect but his knowledge was bad
As to how to salute, so they say.
His coat was bedecked with ribbons galore
KBE, CSI, DSO,
All these had he earned, through the horrors of War,
How could he expect them to know?

Imagine his feelings when prancing along,
Coming nearer and nearer, he spied
The Lord Sahib, attended by one 'aide de cang'
Who were both of them riding astride.
With his old fashioned courtesy (I wish it were mine)
He lifted his cap from his head,
'That comes from living in old Palestine'
Was what the Viceroy said.

A chance not to be missed, said the d--d MSU
Here's a General going astray,
Though he is a big swell, I'll jolly well see
He salutes in the military way.
So a note did he send, by hand, toute-de-suite,
To the General who perhaps did not know,
But the sinner's reply, couched in language so neat,
Was considered a quid for his quo.

The incident's closed, all's well that ends well,
Further action unnecessary, quite,
But I'm glad his reply was not 'Go to H-ll
Whatever I do must be right.'


*Nita to Ralph*

June 23rd, 1920                          Wallaroy, Sydney, N.S.W.
                                         [The home of the Walkers]

My own Darling,

We are all enjoying the Prince's visit immensely, and I have been out every night since Wednesday, 16th, and have still two more dances to go to, so it is just as well that you are not here! I think nine dances running would just about kill you.

The Prince is indefatigable, he dances every night; last Sunday he went up country and returned on Monday night at 11 p.m., he went straight to the Tony Henderson Dance from the Station; on Tuesday he went to the gala performance at the theatre, and came on to the Knox's dance somewhere about 1 a.m. Last night he was at a big Ball given at the Town Hall by members of the Queen's Club, and at midnight took about twelve couples back with him to Government House, sent for the *Renown* band and they danced there till all hours.

He hates formality, and when he goes to dances beyond saying how do you do and good bye, takes no notice of his hostess and refuses to have anybody presented. He won't go into supper form-ally either, and sit-down suppers appear to be extinct. No one has more than stand-up light supper going, this is what he likes best. He has danced the whole week with Molly Little, Rosie Lamsden and a Miss Bell from Coochin, Queensland. To my amusement, he tapped me on the shoulder as I was dancing past him on Tuesday, at the Knox's dance, and said, 'I say, can I have the next dance?' I called out I should be delighted, nearly collapsed with shock; he won't dance with anyone taller than himself, so I am afraid Anne won't have much of a chance; he really is rather an *enfant gâté*, and though he does his duty magnificently most of the day, insists on being allowed to do as he pleases at dances. He is very unpunctual and so are all his staff, he never turns up anywhere on time.

To go back to my dance: we hopped round together and then sat out and had a long heart-to-heart talk on the subject of his visit to India. Poor boy, he was so natural and human about it, he said to me quite frankly, 'Look here, Mrs Verney, I am looking forward immensely to visiting India, but I *don't want* to go there next year. I really don't think I shall be fit for it, this tour has been much more of a strain than anyone realises. I am only going to have a month in England and how can they expect me to recoup in that time; you know what it will be like, I shall be spending the whole time preparing for the visit to India, interviewing people in connection with the visit and seeing to 101 things of that sort, and I haven't seen my home or my family properly for six years. Oh it's rotten luck, people seem to think because I am Prince of Wales I haven't got human feelings, but I love my home, it means more to me than to many people, we're such a happy family and here I am twenty-six tomorrow and I hardly know England'. His eyes almost filled with tears, and I murmured 'you poor boy, it's an abominable shame'. But he could not stop and let out a lot of pent-up feelings. 'No one knows', he went on, 'what acute homesickness I feel; some of my staff may guess but not one realises how I long to live just a quiet life for even a week. I haven't been out of sight of my staff for years.

'Just imagine how you'd feel, always conscious that you're before the public eye; never a second to call your own; it's a strain, a terrible strain, and that is why I do not want to go to India next year. I won't do myself justice, for to make the tour a success I must put lots of pep into everything I say and do. I can't work up that pep in a month – it's an Americanism, but it illustrates what it means, it's just that essential difference between the human being and the dummy. I can go ahead for years as a dummy, bowing right and left like a mechanical figure, but if I've got some pep in me I can be human, say the right word to a wounded man or impress my personality on an Audience as I am speaking. Well I don't suppose there is much chance of my getting out of it, but do impress upon your husband if he has anything to do with my tour that I DON'T WANT TO SEE SIGHTS. I want to see and MEET people, that is what I am touring for, and any spare time in the day I should so much prefer to ride or play squash. I don't play polo but I love riding and hunting beyond anything; if I could get a little hunting in India it would make up for missing it at home.

'I'm a rotten shot, which is a nuisance because my father is such a good one and people think I should take after him, but I've not had a chance, have I? But anyhow' and his eyes twinkled, 'I can ride better than he can, though it's not saying much!! Tell him also to let me have a certain amount of free time each day to amuse myself in, and of course I like to dance every evening; it helps to keep me fit'. I told him I was afraid there was no squash court at Delhi, only tennis courts. 'Oh well, I can ride. I'm not frightfully fond of tennis but I'd like to ride every day and a horse that is a bit of a handful; none of your tame gee-gees.'

He again harked back that it was rotten that he should be sent off so soon to India. 'My people think I can do all the resting I want in the *Renown* between Ports. The *Renown*', he repeated in a scornful voice; 'how can a fellow get relaxation for tired nerves, hemmed in by a huge staff on a ship? If I could only spend that month in London as I pleased,' he almost wailed, 'it wouldn't be so bad, but I know exactly what it will be like, and then to leave dear old England just when hunting is starting, oh, I can't bear it.' He was such a boy, I felt I should like to sit down and cable straight away to the King and the Cabinet what I thought of them all, taxing a boy's strength like this, for he had four very strenuous years at the front, and Canada and America on top of Australia thanks to its democratic tendencies called for so much more effort than even they did.

Your very own

Nita

*Ralph to Nita*

July 5th, 1920                                   Viceregal Lodge, Simla

My own Darling,

I was much amused by Eric Hoare. I had put in orders about the dance 'No Supper will be served in the Council Room after the dance'. Jordan came up to me during the evening with a broad smile and asked if he was to carry out Capt. Hoare's order about supper; I asked what it was and Jordan said, 'Supper for twenty-four in the ADCs' room'!! I said certainly not, but that he might prepare supper there for ten which was for five ADCs with one friend each!! I tackled Eric about it and said I was glad he was so careful to carry out the orders of the MSV about no supper being prepared in the Council Room, and that it was entirely my mistake that I had not mentioned anything about supper for twenty-four in the ADCs' room.

I forgot if I told you we have had a mutiny in the Connaught Rangers, quartered at Solon and Jutogh, owing to the 'present state of Ireland'. They have been quite orderly except for one case where the mutineers rushed the guard of their own regiment who shot two of them and killed them; about 200 were really concerned in it, and the leaders have been sent to Lucknow under escort.

The mutineers issued rather an amusing notice to the General Officer Commanding the Ambala brigade, saying that they would not be prepared to do any work or attend any parade except the parade next Saturday for the purpose of drawing their pay!!

Another big case I have had to deal with lately is the pay of the offices of the PSV and MSV. About six weeks ago the Government of India offered us a rise of 15% on the present scale of pay in these two offices as a result of demands from us. Hignell wanted to accept it straight away but I refused to do so until I knew what was to be the new scale of pay in Government Secretariats, which was to be issued at the end of May. As a result of our waiting, we have now been offered a rise of 25% and I am now going into the whole question to decide if I will accept that, which I expect I shall do, but they have told us they cannot ante-date more than three months because that is their invariable rule, yet, in their own orders about their own Secretariats, I find they ante-dated their own scale of pay from the middle of June to December 1st, 1919, no less than seven months, so I am going to fight them on that point.

Your own husband

Ralph

July 6th, 1920                                        Viceregal Lodge, Simla

My own Darling,

There is one thing HRH will be spared in this country, and that is shaking hands with thousands of people, but as regards his visit to Delhi there are so many official visits from Indian Chiefs which he must receive and pay, as well as the functions which must be done, that it will not be easy to give him a whole morning or afternoon to himself. He is to receive, and pay, a call on all the Indian Princes whom he is not going to see in their own states. I am afraid there is no getting away from that, and the first afternoon, and second morning and afternoon have been given up to that'; but his first morning is blank after his official arrival. The second morning is also given up to these official visits, if there are any who have not been able to be got in before.

The present idea is that HE should go to Bombay, go onboard to lunch with HRH and will then return straight away by train, leaving Sir George Lloyd to receive the Prince when he lands officially in Bombay. The Viceroy's train will be run right onto the Mole in the harbour. J.B. Wood, Worgan and I had a meeting the other day to discuss questions of escorts, etc. We have got another meeting of the general committee on August 17th. I am off to Delhi on Sunday week with Worgan, Harvey and John, and we shall get a good deal settled then I hope.*

Our ADCs' fancy dress dance took place last night and was most admirably done. I took HE and Her Ex. and they were received at the entrance of the club tennis court by the five ADCs dressed in the old uniforms of 100 years ago, with scarlet tail-coats, high stocks, white breeches and white stockings, a gold sword belt across their chests with a light old-fashioned sword, and of course white wigs with a small pigtail tied with black ribbon; they looked awfully nice. The dresses were really excellent and would have done credit to any fancy dress ball at the Albert Hall!

Your own husband

Ralph

*Sir John Barry Wood (1870–1933). Political Secretary, Governor of India 1914–22; Resident Kashmir 1923–27.

Brigadier-General Rivers Worgan (d1936) had served in the Third Afghan War. He was Military Secretary to the Duke of Connaught during his tour in India 1920–21; Military Secretary to the Prince of Wales during his tour in India 1921–22; Military Secretary to the Viceroy of India 1923–26.

July 26th, 1920                                    Viceregal Lodge, Simla

My own Darling,

Yesterday afternoon your long letter of the 23rd June and also your letter of the 26th June arrived, and I was most awfully interested in all you tell me about the Prince of Wales. Certainly, from your account it looks as if there is quite a possibility of his visit to India being postponed for a year, but if this is to be done I do hope they will not wait until he gets home because it is quite certain to be misinterpreted by the extremists in India. Gandhi and his party are starting their policy of non-cooperation on August 1st; if the Prince's visit is cancelled about two months later, Gandhi and Co. are sure to claim that they have frightened the Prince from coming to India.

Besides this, we are of course spending a lot of money, and I do think we ought to be told as soon as possible if this visit is going to be postponed; after what you have told me, I rather hope it will be postponed, but I doubt if the King will be anxious to agree to this, unless it is necessary for the Prince's health. Your programme of dances would most certainly have finished me; I was getting quite nervous about you, knowing all the dances and gaiety which you must have had.

As regards dancing, he will get quite a lot of informal dancing at V.R. Lodge, in fact every night he is there except Sunday, and the levee and State Ball. I do not think that HE would at all like that he should go to the club when we have built this new ballroom entirely for his visit; it rather detracts from his excuse of being overtired, etc., when you tell me of his taking back about twenty couples to Government House after the dance at the Town Hall, sending for the band from the *Renown* in order to continue dancing again till any hour in the morning. Nobody can expect to last at that rate!! I am not surprised to hear of his nerves being all on edge, he sounds as if he was burning the candle at both ends and in the middle as well!!

Your own

Ralph

July 30th, 1920                                    Viceregal Lodge, Simla

My own Darling,

Nothing is known yet in India about the Prince's visit being off; we have sent home a draft communiqué for approval. The *Morning Post* published the fact that the visit was postponed, and Reuters got it from Australia that the visit might have to be put off, for a short period, because of the great strain entailed on the Prince's health by his Australian Tour. We published a thing in Reuters yesterday, to say that nothing was known yet officially about the report in the *Morning Post.*

It has now got to be decided what ought to be done in India, this winter, about the opening of the legislative assemblies. Personally, I am strongly in favour of the Viceroy making a sort of Grand Tour and opening them himself, because I think it is important that these functions should not be allowed to fall flatter than can be helped. Because HE has been so closely associated with the Reform scheme, it would be very good for him to perform the inauguration ceremony, because it would be an excellent opportunity for him to go round and say good bye to the various Capitals before his departure.

I think the departure of this Viceroy is rather different to the ordinary departure of an outgoing Viceroy because it really means, for good or for bad, the end of the old regime in India. The new

Viceroy will have to begin governing India from a different stand-point.

Another thing Her Ex. wanted to do was to keep the Dufferin office open in Simla this winter, and let that house in Cavalry lines in Delhi, to one of these Indian princes coming for the visit of the Prince of Wales, for 5,000 Rs. for a fortnight. Heard told me about this, and I absolutely stopped it as I thought it was gross profiteering at the expense of one of the Indian Princes; we practically order these Princes to come to Delhi, then we profiteer at their expense. I told Heard that we had already had complaints of this nature and that if Her Ex. was allowed to do that, it would absolutely tie the hands of the Viceroy who would not be able to drop on anybody else for doing the same, if his own wife did it; it made no difference at all, really, that it was for the benefit of the Dufferin office. I told Heard to put the whole matter before HE. The only reply he got from HE was that Heard was to do exactly what I advised about it!!!

There is a song in the *Pirates of Penzance*, 'the lot of the police-man is not always a very happy one'; the MSV might well be substituted for the policeman!! However, there have not been any rows over these questions, and Her Ex. never meant me to know anything about her scheme about the Dufferin Office.

Very much love,<br>
Your own

Ralph

August 10th, 1920　　　　　　　　　　　Viceregal Lodge, Simla

My own Darling,

Tonight we have got a big dinner party here, with the following Maharajahs: Bikanir, Scindia, Patiala, Maler Kotla and the Rao of Cutch, coming in afterwards. Jardine is staying here, and is coming to lunch with me today. Boothby leaves at the end of this week. I do not think I shall ask anybody else to stay, as I am expecting Aubrey Metcalfe on the 22nd, which is only a week later, and he may be with me for some time, but I do not know what his plans are.*

Anne is going off to Poona on the 23rd, and is not coming back till the Lloyds come here on October 8th. I am afraid Anne is really fed up with her family; in fact she sent me a note this morning, asking me to arrange her journey on that date, as she could not stand her family any longer. Poor old Heard came to me the other day and said he did not know how he was going to carry on, Her Ex. was so difficult. However I told him my experience was that everybody gets difficult towards the end of the Simla season, and that he was not to worry about it. I believe it was about the Lady Chelmsford maternity ward; I told him about the bungle. I gather the committee are so fed up about the whole thing that they intend to drop the scheme altogether, for the present. Her Ex. was keen to get it started during her time, so that her name might be associated with it.

Your own husband

Ralph

*William Ellis Jardine (1867–1944) was Resident at Gwalior and Baroda 1912–24.

# CHAPTER ELEVEN

In August 1920 it is decided the Duke of Connaught will visit India instead of the Prince of Wales. The start of farewells to the Viceroy who left Simla on October 20th and returned to Delhi after visiting Assam. Nita and family return to Delhi on 15th December. On December 21st the Viceroy pays a final visit to Gwalior.

On January 10th, 1921 Ralph is in Bombay to meet the Duke of Connaught and his staff, with tremendous ceremonial meetings with the Chamber of Indian Princes and Legislative Assemblies. The Duke of Connaught finally leaves Delhi on February 15th. The Viceroy goes to Calcutta for a final visit and then back to Delhi. Nita and family leave for home on March 17th with the Viceroy departing from Delhi on March 29th, 1921.

August 14th, 1920            Viceregal Lodge, Simla

My own Darling,

A wire from the Secretary of State came in this morning to say that the Duke of Connaught will come out to India this winter, instead of the Prince of Wales, for the Delhi part of the programme. A public and official announcement will be made, probably this evening, about it. HE is seeing Vincent and Sir J. Wood at 3 p.m. today.

The official announcement will say that it is owing to the Prince's health that he is not able to come this year but that he will come next year, if his health permits. At any rate, we have at last got something definite to go on, and we can now start making plans for next winter and decide what HE is going to do about going or not going round, to open these other legislative Councils.

HE has just been in and says he wishes me to attend this meeting this afternoon; he told me Montagu has upset the programme again by suggesting that the Duke should arrive in Delhi, to do the programme, on January 1st instead of as already arranged in February. Also, that he should go to Calcutta, Bombay and Madras and perhaps the local Governors. HE is awfully sick about this and we shall discuss it this afternoon.

No more time for more,
Your own

Ralph

August 14th, 1920            Viceregal Lodge, Simla

My own Darling,

The proclamation about the Prince not coming out, and about the Duke coming instead, will be published here on Wednesday. The Secretary of State wired to suggest that the Duke should open all the legislative Councils, but the Viceroy is very much opposed to him doing that, chiefly because it would mean him practically doing the tour which the Prince was going to do, and then much the same tour being done by the Prince the following winter; this would put the Country and a different Government to enormous expense.

What the idea here is that the Duke should do the Delhi programme, but that the rest of his time in India should be spent in
paying private visits to those of the Maharajahs whom he knows
well, like Scindia and Bikanir.

J.B. Wood told me that Maffey wanted to come out with the Duke,
but that if the Duke is only to do the Delhi programme, J.B. thinks
it quite unnecessary that Maffey should come, but I shall be
surprised if he does not do so, from what I know of him!! Failing the
Prince of Wales, I think Maffey will put up with the Duke of C.
quite gladly; what do you think? Of course this means altering the
whole plan of my camp in Delhi, but I am trying to get the Government of India to agree to allow those estimates which I had such
trouble over last winter, to stay as they are. It will only mean that
the Viceroy will have the benefit of everything this winter, and that
everything will be there absolutely ready for when the Prince does
come. J.B. quite agreed with me this afternoon, so I hope we may
persuade Hailey to do so too, between us. We are to have a meeting
about this quite early next week.*

I forgot if I told you that my new scale of pay for the MSV's office
has been approved by the Secretary of State. Most of the members
of my office get a rise in pay of 30% from last April 1st. Devine
goes from 660 Rs. to 800 Rs. per month, de la Hey up to 400 Rs.
and so on right down to the champrassis; it has meant a great deal
of work for me this summer as I have not had Parsons to help
me over this, and Devine is absolutely useless, he really knows
nothing, and I think is an absolute fool. If he were not resigning
soon I would not have agreed to give him 800 Rs. a month, but it
makes a difference to his pension, but he is not worth that salary
in my opinion. De la Hey is much more use to me than Devine is. I
now do all my work with the various departments direct, with the
heads of each department such as Burns, the treasurer, de la Hey
for tours, etc.

The internal situation in India is not good in my opinion. I
believe myself that the feeling between Europeans and Indians is
really acute, and I think that this is largely due to Montagu's
speech in the House of Commons. I do not think it will be possible
for Montagu to come out here as Viceroy, his reception by the
European community would be so frightfully hostile. I never did
think he had any chance of being appointed Viceroy, but I am sure

it is now impossible. HE told me this morning that he had heard
from home that Lloyd George had seen a private deputation, from
the House of Commons, who asked for Montagu to be sacked at
once. L. George said he could not do that so soon after the Dyer
debate, but that Montagu would be relieved of his post as Secretary
of State for India in about three months' time. HE does not wish
this to happen because he says he knows Montagu so well now that,
with all his faults, he thinks it would be easier for him to carry on
with Montagu to the end of his time.

Gandhi is preaching non-cooperation, and today mentioned that
this policy was to be pursued in connection with the visit of the
Prince of Wales; there is no doubt about it that, when the news that
he is not coming is announced, Gandhi and his party will hail it as
a triumph. I feel this will be inevitable and very unfortunate, but it
cannot possibly be helped. Vincent quoted this at the meeting
today, and said that it was very unfortunate that the Prince's visit
has had to be cancelled, though he felt bound to say that he felt
that the non-cooperation policy of Gandhi might have been more or
less successful in Bombay and Lahore, though not in Calcutta or
Delhi. Gandhi is being carefully watched by the Government of
India who are most anxious to avoid making a martyr of him, but if
he goes too far he will be dealt with all right, you may be sure of
that.

I am glad you are pleased about my CIE. It was very nice of your
people to send me a cable, everybody was very kind about it; yes, I
bet Mrs Maffey is pretty sick at not being made a Lady!! I should
have been more sympathetic about it if he had stuck to HE to the
end of his time, though personally, of course, I am jolly glad he did
not do so. Hignell is a very different person to work with, and the
difference has been very marked over this new pay scheme of our
two offices. Maffey refused point blank to work with me over it, and
insisted on the two offices going up to the Government of India
with two schemes; luckily he left before this was done. Hignell
and I worked out a joint scheme together which we sent up to
the Government of India under our joint signatures, and it has
worked admirably. I begged Maffey to allow this to be done, but he
definitely refused, saying that the scale of pay in his office had
nothing to do with the MSC's office and vice versa. Hignell took
exactly the opposite point of view, and said that both the offices

worked for the benefit of HE and that what affected the one was bound to affect the other.

Anne is again hard at it!! though I am glad to say she is confining her activities to V.R. Lodge, but she very obviously means to marry Donough before leaving India; the same old thing having him to tea up in her room, etc., etc., it makes me quite sick. Her Ex. encourages it for all she is worth, whatever she may have said to Joan when she was here.

Very much love, my own darling,

Ralph

*William Malcolm, 1st Baron Hailey (1872–1968) was then a Member of the Executive Council of the Governor-General in the Finance and Home Departments. He later became Governor of the Punjab (1924–28) and United Provinces (1928–30).

*Ralph to Nita*

August 16th, 1920                              Walloroy, Sydney

My own Darling Heart,

I have missed you most dreadfully lately. I was at Yaralla for ten days and it was so full of memories; the children were in our room – it seemed so odd to see all three jumping about in that bed where we jumped about so happily only eleven years ago!! Do you realise, I wonder, that it is eleven years ago today since you proposed to me? I think I shall go down and sit on the sofa and shut my eyes! Kathleen, as you have doubtlessly heard by now, has a fine son, he weighted 10½ lbs. and is a monster; poor child, she had a rotten time as usual.[1]

The Prince is back in Sydney, he got back on Saturday morning. On Friday night I got a telegram, 'Am desired by HRH the Prince of Wales to invite you to dinner on board *Renown* Saturday 8 p.m., please reply by wire, Dudley North.' It was a bombshell; of course I wired back yes and found myself one of a small party of twenty, in fact the chaperone, all the rest being very young girls.

I went up to Yaralla after breakfast, with Col. Grigg, Nell Campbell and Molly Owen and found Telford Simpson, Aylmer Maxwell, the twins, E.C.W. there waiting the rest of the guests.[2]

At 5.30 HRH came up by launch with Admiral Halsey, Lord Louis Mountbatten, Mr Billyarde Leake and a Mr Packenham from the *Renown*; they all raced round the garden, then HRH went and played squash and we all got dressed for dinner. He and the others changed and we went into dinner at 8, a party of twenty. I arranged the table and put him between E.C.W. and Molly Little. He talked to her nearly the whole time, George sat near and kept him in fits with his stories, and afterwards they became so hot that he took him up to his bedroom and gave him the choicest ones there. E.C.W. had a pianist and HRH brought all his own jazz stand, drums, etc., and he or one of his staff played them the whole time; a huge difference, the piano without them sounds so flat.[3]

We danced hard until 11.30. I thought then that it was beginning to fizzle a bit, so I asked the old Admiral to come and be dressed up; he is always ready for a rag. I fixed him up, and he came into the drawing-room and did a nautch dance, then I took Lord Louis and dressed him up; he came bounding up to my bedroom and sat round while I pulled open drawers and cupboards. He went down and gave a very good copy of a tummy dance, then I dressed up Mr Billyarde Leake and he did a clever copy of a wretched woman who does a classical dance, at the Wentworth, in nothing but a mask and a bit of tulle over her bust and between her legs, a real disgrace to a respectable show.

Then I whispered to the Admiral 'come and be leader in Follow the man from Cooks;' he was all for it, he is a terrific ragger. We started off with a tail of twenty, he led us upstairs under all the beds, over them, through the sheets, down the banisters, finally under the dining-room table, the servants all gaping with amazement. The Admiral was first, then Colleen Hixson, myself, Lord Louis and the Prince close on my heels; we finally ended in Col. Grigg's bedroom where the most terrific scrimmage began, nineteen of us in a small bachelor's room, doors locked, lights out, all the bedclothes on the floor, HRH underneath, struggling to get Halsey down, Ned Grigg almost smothered in mattress, several girls on top of him. At first none of us liked to touch the Prince, but we soon followed Halsey and Griggs' lead and either took sides with him or Halsey; sponges, wet towels flew everywhere, and from getting congested we streamed out into the hall. HRH and party went upstairs, Halsey's party remained below and fun waxed fast and furious, the hall and everyone in it got wetter and wetter; at one time I found HRH and Molly Little and Dorothy Lumsden under Eadith's bed and ducked them all with sponges in retaliation, because I went downstairs, lured old Halsey out of the dining-room for HRH to duck with a jug of water and got most of it down my back; when I got upstairs again, he was most apologetic and got a big towel and scrubbed me dry; how you would have hated it. Ned Grigg loved it and so did all the party; HRH told them he enjoyed it more than anything he had done since he had been out.

Best love,
Your own

Nita

[1]The home of Dame Eadith Walker

[2]Captain (later Admiral Sir) Dudley North (1881–1961) had commanded the battle-cruiser *New Zealand* at the Battle of Jutland. He was Extra Equerry to the Prince of Wales during tours to Australia, India, Japan, Africa and South America.

Lt-Col. Edward Grigg (1879–1955) was Military Secretary to the Prince of Wales during tours of Canada, Australia and New Zealand. He was created Baron Altrincham in 1945.

E.C.W. = Dame Eadith Walker

[3]Admiral Sir Lionel Halsey (1872–1949) was Chief of Staff to the Prince of Wales during tours of Canada, Australia, New Zealand, India and Japan. He was Comptroller and Treasurer to the Prince of Wales 1920–36.

Later Earl Mountbatten of Burma (1900–79), last Viceroy of India.


*Ralph to Nita*

October 15th, 1920                          Viceregal Lodge, Simla

My own Darling,

Our full dress investiture last night was quite a success. J.B. Wood got ill again yesterday morning, so George Ogilvie had to do it. I ran it on the same lines as last year and had two pages for the Viceroy who was in robes. We had about eighty decorees of which I was one, getting my CIE from HE. Amoradat told me as I was going with him to the station this afternoon, that at lunch they were discussing the Investiture and HE said that there was only one officer who made his bow really smartly and properly and that was his own Military Secretary!!*

I had a little bit of a crisis two days ago over Biddy. I forget if I told you that she first accepted Bikanir's invitation to go there when HE goes, then she came into my office and asked me to cancel it, both for herself and Sheeper. Two days ago when I was in Her Ex.'s room and she was there, she calmly remarked, 'Oh Ralph, I think I shall join Pa's train at Delhi and come to Jodhpur and to Bikanir'!!! I told her quite straight that she had not been asked to Jodhpur, and that I had cancelled her visit to Bikanir at her own request; she did not say anything, but after lunch just told HE that she had arranged to join him in Delhi and go to Jodhpur and Bikanir with him.

I rather suspected what she was up to, so asked HE next morning if Biddy had said anything about her plans. 'Oh yes,' said HE. 'she told me she is coming to Jodhpur and Bikanir with me.' On which I talked most frankly to HE and told him what had happened; of course he knew nothing about it and told me I was to write to Biddy and say that it certainly could not be arranged, and that he would have told her so himself had he known that she had at first accepted, and then refused, the invitation already. So I wrote to young Bid and told her that Jodhpur was off and that if she wanted to go to Bikanir she had better arrange it herself, quite independently of the Viceroy's party, as I was not going to do it for her. I also tackled Her Ex. about it because she was trying to back up Bid. When Her Ex. tried to make excuses for her, saying she was only an irresponsible child, I said I thought it was quite time for her to grow up!! However HE was most awfully good about it, and when I said I was not going to be bounced like that by Biddy because she happened to be the Viceroy's daughter, he said 'my dear Ralph you're perfectly right, and as you're responsible for making all these worrying arrangements for the family always, you are to do whatever you think right about it,' and he repeated the same thing again that afternoon in my office. It was so typical of the family for Biddy to go behind my back to HE and simply tell him she had arranged to go to Jodhpur, that I thought it would teach her a lesson; she has been much spoilt by Her Ex. here for the last three months, and does not realise she is now coming to V.R. Lodge as a guest. I am afraid the ADCs find it most difficult to be polite to her and they none of them can stick Sheeper.

Tomorrow night we sit down about ninety-five to this dinner to the Chief, and then we have the public departure of the Viceroy today week; by this time next week I shall have said goodbye to Simla.

Very much love, my own darling

Ralph

*Lt-Colonel Sir George Ogilvie (1882–1966) was then Deputy Secretary in the Foreign and Political Department of the Government of India. He later (1929–31) became Resident in Kashmir.

*Ralph to his mother*

October 19th, 1920                          Viceregal Lodge, Simla

My dearest Mother,

I am most interested to hear the electric light has been actually installed at Claydon. You do not say if the whole house is lit with electric light, if so it must have cost a pretty penny to put in; where does the money come from? I only hope Harry is not running the place into debt, more than it is already.

It is most awfully kind of you to wish me to have the furniture from the flat when your lease is up, I am sure it will be most useful to us though I have not the very faintest idea what my future plans will be. I have now applied officially to be transferred to the home establishment of my regiment on vacating this appointment; one great advantage of this is that if I am transferred, Nita and the family will be given 'entitled' passages back to England, which will save quite £200. The suggestion is that I should be posted to a home battalion, and should have to try and persuade the commanding officer of whichever battalion I am posted to, that I require some leave. I certainly intend to take some leave, at least three or four months, which I feel I need and think I have deserved, so if there were to be difficulties about it, I shall probably send in my papers. But I should like to have three or four months in which to decide whether to go on soldiering or not. I expect the chances are I shall not want to return to regimental soldiering, but still I do not intend to make up my mind in too much of a hurry. What would you advise me to do?! Follow your old friend Asquith's advice and wait and see; I expect that, for once, would be sound advice.

Very much love, look after yourself this winter and don't go over-weeding yourself.

Your very affectionate son

Ralph

*Ralph to Nita*

November 15th, 1920           Viceregal Lodge, Delhi

My own Darling,

The Tour in Assam was quite successful, but more from luck than good management. I never saw such haphazard arrangements.

Silchar and Sylhet were the two most risky places we had to visit. At 6 p.m. when it was pitch dark, I went round the police outer cordon and found it consisted of four men under an idiot of an Indian sub-inspector, with no lights and no system of passes at all. I at once got some more men put on there and then, but of course this was totally inadequate. I sent for the special Police Officer attached to us in Assam by the Assam authorities and was told he had gone to the club and would not be back for one and a half hours. A second very peremptory message from me brought him hurrying to my room; he was a man called Ballantine. I asked him if he was the special police officer and he said he was, I then asked if he was entirely satisfied with the arrangements and he said yes, I then asked him if in his opinion four men, in the outer cordon on a pitch dark night on a circumference of nearly a mile, was in his opinion quite adequate and I then let him have it for about ten minutes in my very best style. I was absolutely furious; he had never bothered to go round, nor do anything at all.

I had to go straight off to dinner at once; he told me he could get no more men; I told him that if I did not find twenty-five sentries properly posted when I came out of dinner, I should insist on him being sent back to Shillong and should wire a report to Colonel Kaye the head of the CID to which branch he belonged. When I came out of dinner the twenty-five sentries were there all right and I sent Withinshaw, our very good police officer, and Johns round to

see twice during the night. I told Beaton Bell exactly what I had
done, immediately after dinner, and if you please he was very stuffy
at my interference; however, I soon put a stop to that attitude, and
the whole of the rest of the time the arrangements were very much
better. B. Bell was inclined to say that his dear Assamese people
would never do anything wrong, when Silchar and Sylhet were two
of the very worst places for violent meetings in favour of non-
cooperation etc. Barnes, the Commissioner at Sylhet, and Dawson,
the D.C. at Sylhet, were both absolutely incompetent.

I think you will be amused at our new ballroom here, and with
the Duke's camp. I took HE round it this morning and he was
immensely pleased with the arrangements; of course the tents are
not yet finished as regards the furniture and the silk lining, etc. Sir
George Barnes went to see them this morning just before lunch,
and called them 'wicked', meaning they were too extravagant. I
hotly defended this at lunch, and he withdrew the epithet 'wicked'
asking to alter it to 'wonderful'!

The ballroom is huge!

Your own husband

Ralph

*Ralph to his mother*

December 21st, 1920　　　　　　　　　　Viceregal Lodge, Delhi

My dearest Mother,

I am off tonight with the Viceroy to Gwalior, and shall not get
back until the 31st. We are going right out into the jungle near Sipri
and then on to Shoepur, where I was last April,

I had a talk yesterday with General Worgan, Military Secretary to
the Duke of Connaught. I am to go and lunch onboard the *Malaya*
in Madras with the Duke and his party, before he lands on January
10th. The official landing takes place at 4.30 p.m. so I shall have a
good talk with Cromer, Maffey and Dudley North who are coming
out with the Duke, all of whom I know well. I shall enjoy this. I am
to ride in the second carriage just behind the Duke. I shall only be
in Madras two nights and three days, and it means six nights in the

train on the two journeys, and most of my time will be spent in full uniform!!

No new Viceroy yet; it really is the limit and I do not know how I am going to get all the business done in so short a time. Lord Chelmsford was appointed about this time five years ago, but he was on the spot and was able to say personally to Maxwell what he would take over in the way of carriages, horses, servants, staff, etc. I am so afraid, if Winston is appointed, he will say he must have a good holiday first and ask that the present Viceroy be pressed to stay on. HE and I were talking it over this morning, and I told him this and pressed him not to agree to an extension; he said that if it happened, and he was pressed to stay on, he would suggest that Lord Willingdon be asked to act as Viceroy for six months; it could not be less than six months because the new Viceroy could not come out here in the hot weather nor during the Monsoon . . .

*Ralph to Nita*

December 23rd, 1920                    Viceroy's Camp, Sipri

My own Darling,

No cable from the Secretary of State yet about the new Viceroy. I caught Scindia with that marble egg, at lunch today. I pretended to pick a hard boiled egg out of the dish and passed it to him. HE was awfully delighted and we had a good joke against him. We are staying here till the 26th, when we go on to Shoepur.

Very much love, my own darling,
Your own

Ralph

January 11th, 1921                    Viceroy's Camp, India

My own Darling,

I went onboard HMS *Caroline* yesterday at about 3.30 p.m. and met Rowland first, and Dudley North and all the rest of the staff. I was taken in to meet the Duke in his cabin and gave him HE's letters. We landed at 4.30 p.m. and after the address of welcome we drove up in procession to Government House, Cromer and myself being in the Duke's carriage.

He got a splendid reception, and there were huge crowds in the streets who were most enthusiastic. The non-cooperation supporters in Madras had no success yesterday at all, though they tried to do all they could to persuade people not to go near the procession, sending sandwich men round with 'boycott Connaught' written on the boards, etc.

Maffey is very well and just the same; he has brought a car out onboard the *Malaya*, this gets it out free of all cost and not paying duty; he is a marvel at looking after himself!! He asked me, onboard yesterday, almost as soon as he saw me, if I could tell him if it is settled about his going to the NWFP [North West Frontier Province]. I told him I thought it was settled. He then said that of course he would love to go there, but he was so anxious that HE should not be blamed for giving him that appointment as it meant passing over one or two others, and that he would be quite happy to accept something else first, temporarily. I took this to mean that he would much prefer really to act for Dobbs while he is away for six months, and then be free to be appointed to the staff of the Prince of Wales if he comes out next winter. I may be wrong but I got that impression; passing over the heads of other people did not seem to worry him much, a year ago.

When I met the Duke he said what a long time it was since we had seen each other; considering that we had never met before, I gave the only answer possible – namely what an excellent memory he had!! and could only weakly add, 'I am afraid it is a great many years, Sir'!! I like him very much; there is no doubt he strikes one as a very old man, but he looks so nice and has such nice manners and seems to enjoy things immensely still, that I think he will be quite a success.


*Nita to her sister*

January 25th, 1921                    Viceregal Lodge, Delhi

Darling Sissiekins,

Tomorrow we are all going to church at 10 a.m. to hear a wonderful faith healer; he is a man called Hexon or Hichson, just out from home. He cures by laying on his hands and has performed the most wonderful miracles through faith. He is not a Christian Scientist but is preaching in the Church of England every day, drawing thousands of people to hear him, Mohammedans and Hindus and Christians. His cures are too wonderful for words. Yesterday Commander Wood, a sailor I know and dance with, went to him and had five minutes' prayer and then Mr Hichson laid his hands upon him and cured him on the spot of acute deafness he had suffered from for ten years; he had to leave the Navy on account of it. I am going to ask him to cure mine; he is going to Sydney and you must see him. The extraordinary thing is that I went late into the nursery and told Nurse about him, would you believe it she was supposed to be dying from heart disease eight years ago while with the Walkers, and this very same man cured her after all the doctors had given her up. She has never mentioned it, because she thought people would scoff.

The little Walker boy was also dying of meningitis and the doctors had given him up. Mrs Walker sent for this man, and as soon as he laid hands on this child he picked up, and recovered consciousness. He has restored sight, made deformed limbs straight. To look at, he is a rather common, thickset-looking man with thick black moustache, more like a commercial traveller than anything else. His mother found he had this wonderful gift when, as a child, he took the neuralgia away by laying his hands on her face. She recognised it was some divine power and beseeched him to give up his life to healing, which he has done. There is nothing spiritual about him, he is most matter of fact.

John heard me discussing the faith healer and said in a pensive way 'I wish I met him before I had my tonsils out.' He is still inclined to shudder over the thought of that operation, and is dreadfully nervy if he sees a doctor anywhere about.

Best love to you all,<br>
Your loving

Mid

*Ralph to Nita's father*

January 25th, 1921                    Viceregal Lodge, Delhi

My dear Father,

Since writing to you last, I have been down to Madras to meet the Duke of Connaught, and I had a very interesting four days there.[1]

I drove back in the Duke's carriage in the procession, and I also had quite a long talk with him one morning about his Delhi programme and about the state of affairs in India generally. They had bad luck about the weather, as immediately after the public arrival it poured with rain for four days without stopping, which of course meant cancelling all outdoor engagements, such as races, polo, garden parties, processions, etc.

Three days ago my successor and his wife arrived in Delhi; he is a Major Kennedy-Crauford-Stuart in the 127th Baluchi Infantry and his wife is an American. I don't know that, with the best will in the world, I take to him very much, and his wife is dreadfully unattractive, being very badly dressed, very ugly, and with no idea at all of playing the part of a hostess; I am told she has money, and as he only married her a year ago I suppose that had something to do with it. The unfortunate thing is that Lady Reading is very delicate and nearly stone deaf, so she ought to have somebody on her staff who could help her in the social line.[2]

I have had a very busy time indeed with my successor, taking him all over the stables, and showing him all the horses, carriages, etc., as well as giving him all the information I can about the office work; one good thing – he has bought and already paid for all my uniform, and my pony and my saddles. My motor still remains to be sold, but I hope to get a good price for that. I let him have all my uniforms, as well as my pony and my saddles, for £165 the lot; he would have had to spend anything from £200 to £250 on his uniform alone, so I don't think I have been too grasping.

Your very affectionate

Ralph

[1]The Duke of Connaught (1850–1942) was the 3rd son and 7th child of Queen Victoria. He married, 1879, Princess Louise Marguerite of Prussia; Governor-General of Canada 1911–16. His daughter, Princess Patricia, gave her name to Princess Patricia's Canadian Light Infantry.

[2]Lt-Col. Charles Kennedy-Crauford-Stuart (d. 1942) had been severely wounded when commanding the Hood Battalion at Gallipoli. He was Private Secretary to Lord Grey of Falloden 1919–20.

Wife of Rufus Isaacs, 1st Marquess of Reading (1860–1935), who succeeded Lord Chelmsford as Viceroy of India 1921–25. Lady Reading was the daughter of Lord Melchett, the founder of ICI, of which Lord Reading later became President.

*Ralph to Nita's mother*

February 2nd, 1921                                    Viceregal Lodge, Delhi

My dearest Mummy,

Practically all the new appointments on the staff of the new Viceroy have been made now. Hignell, the present Private Secretary, is staying on, also two of our ADCs, Captains Frazer and Harris, both of the Indian Army. I think I wrote to Daddy that my successor and his American wife had been here; they are on their way home now. Lord Reading [the new Viceroy] arrives in Bombay on the evening of April 1st, but does not disembark till the following morning; he will reach Government House about 11 a.m., have a good long talk till lunch time with the present Viceroy; we shall start off in procession from Government House at about 2.30 p.m. and sail about 4 p.m. Lord Reading will be sworn in as Viceroy about 4.30 p.m. and so will close a most interesting chapter, extending over a period of five years. I shall be on leave for five months, and shall then have to decide what to do; at present the idea of Regimental soldiering again is not at all attractive to me, but if nothing else turns up, I may take to that again.

I am still too young to do nothing! My mother is making such preparations for the return of the children. On their way back they are all going to stop with Prince Charoon at the Siamese Embassy in Paris, for a few days, which Nita will enjoy. It is awfully good of Charoon to put them up, but I have known him of course for years, and we stayed with him in Bangkok in 1912. Also I was able to fix up a pretty good tour for his brother in India this last summer, and

I got him treated as a guest of the Government in India, so perhaps Charoon feels that it is partly a quid pro quo!

Yours always affectionately

Ralph

*Ralph to his mother*

February 16th, 1921                        Viceregal Lodge, Delhi

My dearest Mother,

The Duke of Connaught left yesterday afternoon at 3 p.m. I think the whole visit really was a wonderful success, but it has been a very hard time with a great deal of anxiety because the very first evening I had one of the tents, occupied by one of his ADCs, burnt to the ground in a few minutes owing to the fusing of an electric wire, in spite of every possible precaution having been taken. Naturally I was in a state of nerves the whole time after this. However nothing of any kind happened again; we were lucky in having glorious weather the whole time except the last morning, when we had a really bad dust storm with a high wind.

All our functions with the big processions went off splendidly, without a single hitch; our carriage and body guard looked magnificent, all the Duke's staff and the Duke himself were frankly amazed at the camp here, as they had never seen anything like it before. I have had some photos taken of the interiors of the Duke's tents which I must try and send you.

Our State Ball was a tremendous show, something like 1,800 people were there for it, our four large dinner parties at which a total of about 485 people were present, went off well. I dined quietly with the Duke on Thursday night, Colonel Alan Paley of our first Battalion being there, also Col. Pitt Taylor of the regiment, so it made a kind of small Rifle Brigade dinner though some of his staff were there too, but we had a most cheery evening.[1]

The Duke was charming on the morning of the day he left giving me his photo, signed by himself, and a very nice silver cigarette box as a momento of his visit, and saying a lot of nice things. Cromer and the rest of his staff were equally nice and I am glad to say that the visit passed off without the slightest friction between the Duke's staff and ours; quite the opposite, we got on capitally together, a thing which I am told has never been done before!!

The Inauguration of the Chamber of Indian Princes in the Fort was a fine sight. Nita and our guests had very good seats for all the shows and the children went to one or two things, including wonderful illuminations and fireworks in the Fort on Monday evening. A very fine sight was the laying of the foundation stone of the All India War Memorial, out at New Delhi. The Duke, The Viceroy and the C-in-C followed by their three Military Secretaries, inspected the Colour Parties and old Indian Officers drawn up on three sides of a square, then the Duke addressed the troops and laid the stone; after that the Colour Parties marched past the Duke at ten paces interval, all officers saluting each Colour as it passed – there were over sixty different regiments represented. The Colour Party then went on and lined both sides of the road along which the Duke and the Viceroy motored away. I was in front of their car and we went very slowly through these lines of lowered colours.

In opening the Legislative Assemblies the Duke made a very good speech, the best part of which was the last two pages when he made a very touching personal appeal, as an old man and as an old friend of India, to allow past differences to be dropped (referring of course to the bitterness over General Dyer, etc) and to work together in close cooperation to make the most of the new Reform schemes which he had come out to inaugurate.

I am bound to confess that Mr Gandhi has had quite a fair success in Delhi in persuading the crowds to boycott the visit. I happened to be taking Cromer out to New Delhi on Sunday afternoon and, quite by chance, we were passing the Fort abut 3 p.m. on Sunday afternoon just when Gandhi was coming back from opening a school or something; there were thousands of people round his carriage, it was quite impossible to pass so the only thing to do was to pull up in the road, short of where he was going to turn up the Chandi Chowk, and wait till he had passed. The crowd was quite orderly but it was a very sad contrast to the crowds assembled to see the Viceroy and the Duke go to the Fort, though Gandhi was only in an obviously old Victoria and the Viceroy and the Duke were in the State carriages with full escorts, etc. I am glad to say the Duke did not see this; it was intensely interesting but made one realise how dreadfully few people had really turned out to welcome the Duke. However we could not help that; everything for which we were responsible went off well.

I am off to Calcutta on Saturday with Their Ex.s, then I have to go across to Bombay for two days when I am going to stay with the Admiral, Sir Hugh Tothill, in order to say good bye to the Duke on behalf of the Viceroy. I hope to bring back to Delhi with me Mrs Balfour, Daisy Lascelles that was, Lady Lloyd's sister. I have to go to Jammer on March 4th, returning to Delhi on the 6th, as the Viceroy is going to invest in Full Durbar the Maharajah of Kashmir with his full powers; that will be our last little tour. I shall be here then till the 29th when we finally leave.[2]

We have a full dress investiture on 17th March, in the new ballroom. Sir Edward and Lady Maclagan (he is the Governor of the Punjab) are coming to stay for a couple of days about the 19th, after that pack up![3]

Very much love,
Your very affectionate

Ralph

[1]Colonel Alan Paley (1887–1950) joined the Rifle Brigade in 1897, three years before Ralph.

Later General Sir Walker Pitt-Taylor (1878–1950). Walter Pitt-Taylor joined the Rifle Brigade in 1899.

[2]Admiral Sir Hugh Tothill (1865–1927) was Commander-in-Chief East Indies 1919–21.

Margaret (Daisy) Lascelles had married first, 1867, Max Livingstone Learmonth. He d. 1912. She married, 2ndly, 1914, Melville Balfour. Her sister Blanche was married to Sir George Lloyd.

[3]Sir Edward Maclagan (1864–1952) was Governor of the Punjab 1921–24.

March 22nd, 1921                                   Viceregal Lodge, Delhi

My dearest Mother,

I suppose this is my last letter from this address to you. I have had a wireless from Nita saying that they are settling all right onboard the *China* though I am afraid they had rather a hot journey down to Bombay, but Nita found many friends onboard and was sitting at a table with Lady Ennismore who came and stayed in Delhi with Daisy Balfour for a few days.*

I am leaving no less than seventeen cases of things here in Delhi, silver, books, pictures, etc. etc. It is no good bringing them all home, and having to pay storage there, when I can leave them here properly stored for nothing; also if, by any chance, I come back to India I shall want them out here in this country. I am sending also a great many cases up to Simla of things to be sold by auction: pictures, books, clothes, any number of toys, a pram, etc. The Viceroy is away for a few days seeing the Kadir Cup, which gives me a chance of looking after my own affairs. The exchange between here and England is so bad just now that I am leaving as much money as I can out here invested in Jute Shares!! When the exchange goes up, which I think it should do in about six months or so, and when my shares do the same which I think they should do in about the same time, I can then sell out and have the money sent home to me. But £1,500 six months ago is now worth about £1,150, so really one simply cannot afford to have one's money sent home just now.

The final public departure takes place actually a week hence at 6 p.m., the train leaving at 6.30 p.m. We had it pretty late in the evening because the temperature in Delhi now is well over 90 in the day time, but I have got an electric fan buzzing away now in my room as I write, and it is nearly 6 p.m. The garden is now looking lovely. I am glad it will be nice when our successors arrive. Having packed up almost everything in this house, I have most of my meals either up at V.R. Lodge or else with Hignell, the private secretary; he very kindly asked me to stay with him for this last week but I preferred to stay on in my own house, as there is still a good deal to do.

Very much love,<br>
Your very affectionate

Ralph

---

*A daughter of 2nd Baron Derwent, married, 1904, Richard Granville, Viscount Ennismore, later 4th Earl of Listowel.

*On his return to England Ralph was invited to accept the appoint-
ment of Secretary to the Speaker*

*Ralph to Nita*

April 25th, 1921                    33 Manor House, Marylebone Road

My own Darling,

No letter from Whitley [the Speaker], but I did not expect one; I
am almost going to dread being given the job now. I feel I shall be so
frightfully strange and at sea in those surroundings for some time. I
shall not leave those letters of introduction until we know more
about our plans. I daresay I shall try and get to Ellin [Claydon
Harry's sister] some time tomorrow, I shall also go and see Rosie
Fellows at the War Office, and one or two other friends.

Very much love, my own darling. Nurse went off from the station
somewhere, I have not seen her again, I gave her a return ticket as
a present.

Your own
Ralph


May 2nd, 1921

My own Darling,

I have had a very busy day in the House, there is such a lot to
learn and so many people to get to know. I met Leslie Wilson who
was most cordial. Mr Whitley wants us both to go to tea next week;
there are various people you must call on next week, Lady Keppel,
the wife of the Serjeant-at-Arms, Canon Carnegie's wife who was
Mrs Joe Chamberlain, he is the Speaker's Chaplain.

I think I shall revel in the work when I get more used to it; my
appointment will be in the papers tomorrow. I lunched at the House
today with Cadogan who has been charming, I want you to meet
him next week, I am glad to say he is staying on with me till
Whitsuntide. I am not going to the House till 10.30 tomorrow
morning, but have got the tailor before that.

Your own

Ralph

# Postscript

Ralph continued as Speaker's Secretary to four Speakers and eight different Prime Ministers, completely revolutionising the duty of Secretary because he brought to this appointment all his experience as Military Secretary.

His service to Parliament was so outstanding that he was Knighted in 1928 and given a Baronetcy in 1946. He finally retired in 1955 when he was seventy-six years old.

Ralph died in 1959 having served his country continuously since he was twenty-one years old.

# *Index*